C000186966

Create Contracts Clients *love*

Design readable contracts clients love with fast (and fun!) workflows

Verity White

'Create contracts clients love — is that even possible?

Verity White knows that it is — she's been there and done that. Her down-to earth, easy to follow steps show you how.

This book should be mandatory reading for all contract writers. Verity rocks. Guided by her book, we can all become the contract rockstar of our organization!'

Helena Haapio, Contract Strategist, Lexpert Ltd and Associate Professor of Business Law, University of Vaasa

'What a refreshing approach to creating contracts!

Read it and loved it because it felt like I was having a really helpful conversation rather than reading a book.'

Melissa Lyon, Executive Director & Experience Designer, Hive Legal

'A sign of true intelligence is the ability to make things simple for others. As professionals, it is surely our duty to make our knowledge and expertise easily accessible and useful. With this book, we have no excuse.

Create Contracts Clients Love guides us on a journey of user-based design and simplification, a journey that turns contracts from instruments of prevention to a source of value and opportunity.

Read it, then use it to escape the trap of the past. Your work, your contracts are just too important to remain in the realms of obscurity.'

Tim Cummins, President, World Commerce & Contracting and Professor, University of Leeds, School of Law

'The digitisation of contracts and consequent disruption of contract life cycle management has never been more topical or important than it is right now.

We're on the cusp of significant change to how we conceive, design and develop contacts. It's a change that will impact every corner of the legal and business marketplace.

Against that background, Create Contracts Clients Love provides a practical, user-friendly guide for all legal practitioners, business professionals and contract managers who are focussed on doing contracts differently – it's timely and important - great stuff, Verity!'

Terri Mottershead, Executive Director, Centre for Legal Innovation (Australia, New Zealand and Asia-Pacific)

'Contracts are the backbone of business. They often establish long-term relationships between two parties. Yet, contracting has long been marred by flaws in drafting, in negotiation, and in management.

Thankfully, there is help. Verity's updated book takes an engaging and holistic look at contracts and proposes relatable and sound tips on how to contract better.

Create Contracts Clients Love is a practical, concise, and fun guide that provides sound advice on client-centric contracting.'

Colin S. Levy, Legal Technology Thinker, Speaker, and Writer, colinslevy.com

'Such a timely and practical guide to simplifying contracts – Verity packs in a tonne of value, original thinking and creativity that will inspire anyone who touches contracts.'

David Bushby, Managing Director, InCounsel

Dedication

This book is dedicated to the undecided and the indecisive. It is possible to find your passion.

About the author

Verity White is a commercial lawyer turned legal innovation expert with a passion for redesigning legal documents, contracts, and processes to be easy to read, easy to use, and jargon-free.

After 10+ years in corporate law land, Verity saw a problem. Too many business owners and lawyers were held back by confusing contracts and clunky legal processes. So, she started Checklist Legal to put her love for problem-solving and fixing things to good use. And to help change the world of contracting for the better!

Now, Verity is a multi-award-winning lawyer, legal innovator, and speaker sharing her love for clear, clever contracts with businesses and lawyers around the world. As an Honorary Senior Fellow at the University of Melbourne, Verity teaches Contract Design for Automation and is helping shape a new generation of lawyers (and contracts!).

When she's not trying to revolutionise the legal industry, you'll find her going all-out for a themed costume party (yes, even on zoom), walking a very cute Cavalier, or mixing up her go-to cocktail, a margarita.

Acknowledgments

Thank you to these legends who gave love, time, and encouragement to make this book happen:

Dean Manners, equally patient, encouraging, and realistic, thank you for bringing treats to my desk, taking me (and Brinkley) for walks, and for being the best lockdown partner anyone could want.

My family (in no particular order!), I am lucky to have several sets of parents, brothers, a sister, and more and I love you all! You are kind and caring and listen to me talking about contracts far more than anyone sensibly should... thank you Anne Fisk, Richard White, Peter Fisk, Kale White, Nicholas Colless White, Tehlia Colless White, Matthew Fisk, Lisa Chandler, Indira White, Fofey White.

Emily Booth, you are what all lawyers should aspire to become: clever, kind, fun, solutions focused, and great on the dance floor. Thank you for talking legals with me.

Helena Haapio and Tim Cummins, thank you for being kindred spirits in contract simplification and consistent sources of inspiration and forward thinking.

Melissa Lyon, Terri Mottershead, David Bushby, Colin Levy, and **Natalie Bryant** for your enthusiasm for innovation and kind encouragement.

Melanie Thomas, thank you for being a general legend and contract design bestie on the (sometimes) lonely road of in house legal innovation.

Jeannie Paterson, you saw me present on contract design and invited me to turn my ideas into a masters level university subject... thank you for your belief and encouragement!

Caitlin Whiteman, thank you for your plain language expertise and editorial skills when you definitely had better things to do.

Lauren Frederiks, thank you for your patience with changes, updates, and middle of the night ideas, you are a graphic designer dreams are made of.

Lauren Stephens, we will be ladies who lunch again soon! Thank you for being a sounding board and editor for my very rough drafts.

Thank you again to the OG book team of Lauren Stephens, Caitlin Whiteman, Emily Booth, Richard White, Pia Chadwick, Lisa Chandler, Anne Fisk, Ryan Hooper, Peter Fisk, Fofey White, Allison Hooper, and of course Beyoncé Knowles ^_^

Digital Resources

This book comes with further digital resources (sweet!).

For templates and checklists, head to: www.createcontractsclientslove.com

Scan the QR code to visit the Create Contracts Clients Love site and access included templates

Copyright

Originally published by Checklist Legal under the title 'Secrets of Productive Contracts, copyright © Checklist Legal, 2017

Electronically distributed version published by Checklist Legal, copyright © Checklist Legal, 2020

Second edition, updated and published by Checklist Legal, copyright © Checklist Legal, 2021

All rights reserved. Please do not reproduce or transmit a copy of this publication in any form without the written consent from the author, Verity White.

ISBN 978-0-645231-0-8

Disclaimer

Verity White is a lawyer, but she is not your lawyer unless you formally hire her under an agreement.

This book is intended for general business purposes only, so please do not rely on it for tailored legal advice. Your situation may be different and the laws of other countries or jurisdictions may mean the information in this book is incorrect for your circumstances.

Please use your common sense and seek professional independent advice if you need it. For a list of free referral services for legal assistance in Australia, please see the Resources section at the end of the book.

Updates for the second edition

In 2017, I was excited to bring my little book baby into the world. Then named 'Secrets of Productive Contracts', I wanted to introduce everyone to my Reverse Sandwich Contract™ concepts and processes.

What happened since 2017 has been amazing and frustrating at the same time.

Both Contract Design and Legal Design are taking a strong foothold in the legal industry. Increasingly more academic literature and top tier law firms are introducing innovation and design thinking into their practice areas. New Law continues to grow and with it the push for value-based pricing to replace the billable hour. There are more technology options than ever, just check out Stanford Law School CodeX Techindex (Techindex). The Techindex is 'a curated list of 1277 companies changing the way legal is done' and is used by some in the legal industry as a way of tracking legal technology trends. The Technindex lists 239 companies under the category of 'Document Automation'. That number just a few years ago was only double digits.

So with all this automation and focus on innovation, lawyers must be living the good life. They must be lying by the pool, clicking a few buttons every now and then to automate another contract before sipping on a cool drink and taking an afternoon nap... right?

Contracts and negotiations are divisive, undermining the cooperation needed for shared benefit.

World Commerce and Contracting

The more things seem to change in the legal industry and the more clients call out for change, contracts themselves seem to be growing more complex. Contracts are large beasts, difficult to tame. We are automating more than ever but we have less time to improve the process or simplify the documents before we automating them.

The continued need for simplification is highlighted by the World Commerce and Contracting (**WCC**) 2020 research into the most negotiated contract terms. WCC runs this research every year, benchmarking the most negotiated terms as reported by their thousands of members around the globe. For the last ten years, limitation of liability has taken the top spot as the most negotiated term, despite the fact it has never reached the top five position as the 'most important' term in a contract.

I teach contract law at Harvard Law School and I can't understand my credit card contract. I just can't. It's not designed to be read.

Elizabeth Warren

And so, with the explosion of tech comes an explosion of complexity. The aim of this updated edition is the same as the first edition; offer practical ideas for contract simplification that go further than just thought leadership or dreaming. Techniques and processes that people from all walks of life can apply to contacts and legal documents to improve their business outcomes and reduce their own stress levels!

That cold and intimidating night back in 2015 still drives me even today. That churning belly feeling that contracts can create is something that we can change!

Together, we can create and automate better contracts!

Contents

The guide to skipping ahead

I encourage skipping ahead and dipping in and out of this book. This matrix will also help for quick reference later if you are looking for a particular section or need a refresher.

SECTION	MINDSET	IT'S ABOUT...	SKIP AHEAD IF...
1. THE BITS AT THE FRONT	Ready for change	A few bits of admin. Good for those who like details.	You've read the book before.
2. THE REVERSE SANDWICH CONTRACT	Useful & usable	Structure your contracts like a reverse sandwich for big productivity wins.	You understand the Reverse Sandwich Contract.
3. A CONTRACT IS NOT A BIT OF PAPER	Think digitally	Think about work & life digitally. See your contract as a tool to map relationships.	You love digital concepts & work paperlessly.
4. BE A LAZY LAWYER	Delegate like a diva	Find minions (robots & people) to do work for you.	You are a diva (or you outsource, delegate & automate like one).
5. TRIPLE O PRODUCTIVITY	Systematise productivity hacking	A quick overview on three levels of thinking to make anything more productive.	You know the three Os of productivity: Obliterate, Optimise, & Outsource.
6. PRODUCTIVE CONTRACT DOCUMENT	Design for readability	Obliterate, Optimise, & Outsource the contract document.	Your contract is easy to read. It's ready for its close-up.
7. SLAPP YOUR CONTRACT	Fine tune document performance	Five key angles to check for contract productivity: Structure, Likeability, Automation, Plain language, & Pictures.	You've already assessed your contract and understand key areas to improve.
8. LOSING LEGALESE	Less Legalese	Let's drop the legalese and go for clarity instead	Your language is already as plain as the nose on your face.
9. MAJOR MAPPING	Complex not complicated	Make the contract process visible by asking key questions & trying different mapping techniques.	You have a black belt in six sigma lean process improvement.
10. PUTTING ALL THE SECRETS TOGETHER	Making productive magic happen	Step-by-step process for making a very tasty (& productive!) Reverse Sandwich Contract.	You're good to go if you know all the secrets & how to put them together.
11. OUTRODUCTION	Go out and do it	Get pumped for the next steps.	You hate goodbyes...
12. THE BITS AT THE BACK	Tools of the trade	Templates, links, & other resources to help you create & automate better contracts.	You want to do it yourself... without help or free resources.

THE BITS AT THE FRONT

MINDSET:
Ready for change

Introduction

Have you ever had multiple thoughts, all at the same time?

I feel sick!

Maybe we could call it off?

What if I miss something?

I could lose thousands of dollars I get this wrong... Is this guy trying to trick me?

I don't want to look stupid!

I feel so dumb...

Is this normal?

All these thoughts rushed through my panicked mind when I walked into a 'casual' meeting with a real estate agent to 'discuss' making an offer on an apartment — my very first attempt at home buying.

I struggled to understand the heavy, two-inch-thick contract in front of me. I panicked and I got frustrated. Even though I am a lawyer, paid to read contracts every day. Despite the fact I spent over three years studying law, had extensive practical legal experience as a paralegal and was practising as a lawyer professionally for five or so years at the time, still I felt confused and bamboozled.

After this moment, I was shocked.

What must legal transactions such as this feel like for people without years of training or a basic understanding of contract law?

Looking back now, that stressful, chilly night in 2015 really pushed me to look at contracts and the law differently.

This book is the result of my own struggles with many complex commercial legalese battles and personal legal frustrations.

By this time, I had already worked hard to create contract efficiencies and was laying the foundation knowledge for the processes and ideas that now form the foundation of this book (and its previous edition, titled Secrets of Productive Contracts). However, something about this particular night and the powerful feeling of helplessness and outrage that lingered spurred me to think about contracts more broadly.

There are at least two major moments in my personal life (so far, I am sure there will be more!) where I struggled to read a relatively everyday contract. The first is the above situation, when I felt ambushed into signing a contract for the purchase of an apartment.

The second was going through a 'de facto divorce', where I needed to divvy up the very same apartment in a legal way.

Even lawyers can't read contracts

As the earlier quote from Harvard Professor Elizabeth Warren shows, even the best, most experienced lawyers struggle with poorly written, large contracts. Does that make you feel better? It made me feel better when I first heard it.

Similarly, when I heard Una Jagose speak at a plain language conference, she described the way she felt about plain language legal writing, in that she it must mean she was stupid because she preferred plain language to legalese.

As the Solicitor General of New Zealand, empowered to make sure the government runs the country according to New Zealand law, it's pretty clear Una Jagose is very smart. Her presentation echoed my own feelings that the smarter option is to simplify legal content.

I've always been a bit inclined towards plain language, but for a long time, it made me think that it meant I wasn't very smart.

Una Jagose

At the same time as we need simpler contracts, we also need simpler processes. Contracts don't just magically sprout from the earth after you plant a legalese seed. Contracts are created by people and processes and business rules. And we often need to simplify these business rules as well as the documents that are created to support them.

When you have a simple contract document and a simple contract process, you will have what I call a Productive Contract.

So what are 'productive' contracts?

Productive contracts are contracts humans can efficiently and easily read, understand, and use. Pretty simple huh?

This book will help you create contracts that everyone can read and understand and actually use.

The world is moving too fast for paper. If your business documents aren't optimised for electronic signatures, digital workflows, and automated processes, you, your clients, and your business will be left behind.

If you want to do more with less, you need to focus on doing the right things, in the right order, and increase your productivity.

If you want to remove the drudgery from document creation, you have come to the right place.

This book is filled with examples of why simplicity will help make you and your contracts more productive, increasing successful outcomes for your business, reducing costs and waste from double (or triple!) handling, giving you back your time, focus for deep work and sanity.

With these secrets, you can generate value so your contracts are always worth far more than the paper they are written on (or the hard drive they are saved on).

Who is this book for?

This book is for anyone who is sick of trying to read ugly contracts and tired of the drudgery of contract admin. This book is written for:

- Lawyers who want to sign up clients faster and help their business clients grow
- legal teams in process driven corporations
- paralegals putting contracts together
- solo lawyers at medium sized companies
- executive assistants chasing signatures
- founders of start-ups and micro-businesses
- procurement specialists and contract managers

Basically anyone who interacts with contract processes or documents and thinks 'There has to be a better way!'.

Hint: There is!

However you interact with contract documents or processes, there are ways to make them more enjoyable, and more productive. And better yet, you don't need a law degree or expensive consultants or mega bucks for an entire new suite of technology.

To make change happen, you need some tenacity and the desire to do things a bit differently.

If you have a passion for productivity and you're willing to talk to people about how they use a contract.

If you want faster, fairer contracts that leave your customers with a positive impression.

If you want your contracts to add more value to the business and to smoothly slide through the approvals process.

...then this book is for you.

Never underestimate the resistance to change from lawyers.

Stephen Poor

This book isn't for everyone

I don't want you to waste your time (or complain to me!) if this book isn't the right fit for you.

It takes a special kind of person to try things differently. Lawyers are not known for being early adopters of new technology or innovation.

After attempting a lean law technology transformation project at a large US law firm, Stephen Poor gave a stern warning to anyone attempting a similar undertaking within the legal industry to expect resistance from lawyers. Not only did Poor explain the enormous push back to any change, he also called out lawyers will often 'describe virtual status quo efforts as revolutionary change.

So perhaps you need to stop for a moment and genuinely ask yourself, are you ready for change?

You, your clients, your team, or your business might not be ready to re-design and digitise the way you work.

Some people aren't ready to see contracts differently. In fact, most people don't like change.

Whilst change can be uncomfortable, I am betting you picked up this book because you have the spark of innovation inside you. I think you know you can make a meaningful change to the people you work with and to your clients and customers. As well as increase your happiness levels at work and stress less about contracts.

If that sounds like you, then you are in the right place!

What you'll need

The key secrets in this book will help you craft more productive contracts to wow your customers and boost your productivity. This book gives you a kick start towards thinking about contracts digitally to craft contracts that combine management of legal risks with powerful productivity and awesome user experiences.

To put the secrets of contract productivity into action you will need:

- a desire to live in the future early
- the ability to encourage people to try new things
- a computer
- a writing program (such as Microsoft Word or Google Docs)
- a short sample contract you want to improve
- if you want to go digital, you'll need access to an electronic signature or automation application

How do you create and automate amazing contracts?

The key tactics of making amazing contracts are distilled in this book for you.

My hope is that this book gives you the mindset, skills and tools you need to remove wasted effort and drudgery from your contracts. Following these tactics, contracts become more productive, faster to create, and easier to manage.

These contract design tactics and tools took years of research, testing and failed attempts to perfect. You don't have to go through all that though (lucky!). You can start using these tools today (yep... today today) to noticeably increase the speed, efficiency and productivity of your contracts.

The busier life gets, the more value there is in simplicity as a point of competitive differentiation

Arkadi Kuhlmann

Key tactics you will learn

As you will soon learn, we should always get the good stuff up front where it's easy to find, so let's get stuck into the key tactics for creating and automating amazing contracts!

1. The Reverse Sandwich Contract

Mindset: Useful and usable | Structure your contract document for the future to get productivity wins on the board, fast.

2. Your Contract Is Not a Bit of Paper

Mindset: Think digitally | Start thinking digitally to see your contract (and life!) for what it really is and what it could be.

3. Be a Lazy Lawyer

Mindset: Delegate like a diva | Learn to automate and outsource. Always lookout for others (human and robot) who can most effectively do each contract task, leaving you to increase your skills in higher value areas.

4. Triple O Productivity for your document and process

Productive contract document

Mindset: Write for readability | Obliterate, Optimise and Outsource your contract document for massive productivity gains. SLAPP your contract into shape. Use the SLAPP system to confirm your contract document is at its productive peak – Structure, Looks, Automation, Plain language, Pictures.

Productive contract process

Mindset: Be curious | Obliterate, Optimise and Outsource your contract process for an ongoing efficiency pay off. Don't put lipstick on a process pig! Fix your contract process and become the contract rockstar of your organisation.

Which contracts can you make more productive?

All kinds of contracts! Because these contract design methods and Reverse Sandwich Contract™ techniques are a way of thinking, not an expensive, bespoke piece of software, the methods apply to all contracts and can help improve any contract in many different ways.

The Reverse Sandwich Contract™ method has a track record of successful with (amongst other things):

- auditing of franchisees
- consulting agreements
- performance warning letters
- franchise agreements
- marketing services
- confidentiality agreements
- letters of intent
- risk assessments
- settlement agreements
- corporate services agreements
- approval processes
- letters of consent
- contract variations
- wholesale service agreements
- marketing release forms
- contract summaries and sign off sheets
- termination letters
- terms of settlement and release
  - ... much more!

If you are just starting out, start with a simple letter or agreement and work from there (see the **List of Low Hanging Contract Fruit**).

These tactics apply to all contracts. All contracts – no matter how complex – can benefit from the contract design and productivity tactics in this book. More complicated contracts can often benefit the most!

Start small and work your way up to the big ones.

Experimenting with contract productivity

When I began experimenting with contract productivity and automation, I was a junior lawyer with no budget.

My friendly, small in-house legal team of six had no money for expensive, custom-built software. We didn't have legal secretaries to complete paperwork. We did have one paralegal. They were doing their best but they were still learning and we were stretched thin.

Then, we didn't even have a paralegal anymore.

I needed to get more contracts out the door and into the hands of willing customers but I had less help than ever. A standard day would look something like this:

- Check tracking on envelopes with the Post Office to see if contracts were delivered.

- Update internal clients who were waiting for basic contracts to either be generated, printed, sent, signed or returned.

- Chase around executives (often interstate) to sign documents.

- Create a cover sheet with internal approvals to assure executives that the contracts were okay for signing.

- Follow up with personal assistants to see whether Directors had signed contracts yet.

- Maintain records of all signed contracts throughout the life of the contract relationship to ensure important dates are not missed.

Basically, it was admin heavy and filled with drudgery. I was drowning in stacks of contracts in the 'to be scanned and filed' pile. Not to mention my poor email inbox, filled with status update email requests, follow up emails, rejected file-size-too-big emails and emails to myself to remember to follow up a contract.

Does that sound familiar? I knew there had to be a better way. So, I started experimenting. As the experimenting began, trends started to pop up across the different contract types.

I started to notice something

As predicted by the Pareto Principle (also known as the 80/20 rule), I started to notice that around 80% or so of a contract wouldn't change for different deals. The 20% or so areas of the contract that did change were typically the real juicy areas: the key details. These key details that changed regularly were often scattered haphazardly throughout the document.

The key details – crucial to the contract relationship's success or failure – were hidden away in definitions, footers, notice clauses, wordy paragraphs, and elsewhere. Hidden deep within the contract was the 20% of key details that often needed to change. And I had to wade through the other 80% to hunt out these key details.

I knew there had to be a better way. So, I started experimenting.

I started to notice more things...

- the less I needed to change in each contract, the faster I could get it back to my internal client.

- the closer together the 20% key details were, the less 'digital distance' (scrolling, clicking, searching, page turning, etc) I needed to cover when creating a contract.

- the more details I could get others to fill in for me, the less time I needed to spend on admin tasks.

- the less mind-numbing admin work I had to do, the better and faster I did high value legal work.

- the faster I did the legal work, the sooner the contract was in the hands of the customer.

- the sooner the contract was in the hands of the customer, the sooner they signed it.

- the sooner they signed, the sooner my company was earning revenue.

- the sooner my company was earning revenue, the sooner my internal clients were earning commissions.

- the more actual legal work I did, the more engaged and excited I felt about my job.

Whilst I had restructured several main contracts to make them easier to handle and far more productive, I knew there was still a missing ingredient. Even with happier clients and less stress, I wanted to get even more done.

I was only just at the tip of the productive contract iceberg.

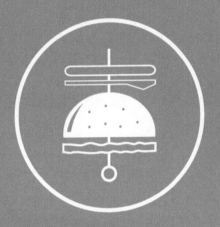

THE REVERSE SANDWICH CONTRACT

MINDSET:
Useful and useable

In most areas of business, usability and user-experience are considered important dimensions of quality. Not so in contract drafting.

Helena Haapio

I'll have the same as sandwich

John Montagu (1718 – 1792), Fourth Earl Sandwich (Kent, England) is said to be the namesake of our tasty lunchtime staple, the sandwich. Before the Fourth Earl Sandwich, a sandwich was just called bread and meat.

The gossip goes that the middle-aged Earl Sandwich loved his card games. During one particularly long gambling session of 'four and twenty hours at a public gaming-table', Earl Sandwich got a little peckish. The Earl would order beef between two slices of bread (apparently, there's no time for knives and forks if you're on a bender).

The Earl's friends started to order 'the same as Sandwich!'

The Earl's friends and gambling buddies saw the wisdom in continuous, cutlery-free betting, so they started to order 'the same as Sandwich!'

Others think this is a bit rough on poor old Sandwich and they put forward an alternative theory. Having become the Earl of Sandwich at just ten years old, the fourth Earl Sandwich led a busy life. The Earl was a workaholic. He would often work long hours. Earl Sandwich was among the first to work through lunch eating a sandwich at his desk. Like our modern habit of eating over the keyboard in front of our computers, the Earl realised a sandwich at one's desk is a handy way to eat and keep working without wrestling with silverware.

We can almost imagine the Earl's subordinates beginning to do their work over lunch just like their boss, their mates walking past and commiserating with them on their workload. 'Pulling a Sandwich, huh? Rough!'.

I like to think it was a combination of both working and gambling (as well as sandwich loving!) that created the name.

What does the earl sandwich have to do with contracts?

A sensible question, I am glad you asked!

Traditionally, a standard contract is structured like a basic sandwich. Simple bread on the outside with the tasty stuff hidden in the middle.

As lawyers and contract writers, we have all copped this. We use precedents our managers and colleagues used. Even though we don't need every clause, we don't delete it because it 'might come in handy' or it 'must be there for a reason'.

If we get excited, sometimes we change the font from Times New Roman to Arial. We might add a few headings. Generally, though, the basic text and structure of contract stays the same; Slabs and slabs of eye-crossing text, designed specifically to confuse and intimidate.

When it comes to contracts, we keep ordering the same old contract sandwich too!

When it comes to contracts, we say 'I'll have the same Sandwich!'. We've used precedents based on precedents from years before, never really challenging the way they are structured.

Why? It seems quicker at the time. It's hard to challenge those in positions of seniority. To borrow a Dr Steven Covey-ism, often we're too busy shoveling the little rocks and gravel these old-fashioned contracts produce to stop and think about the Big Rocks of contract drafting.

This book is here to show you something different. A different kind of contract sandwich. Because you don't have to order the same contract sandwich as everyone else.

What if we all wrote beautiful contracts that everyone could read, understand, and use?

I often like to think about everyone who touches contracts trying to make them better and easier to understand, instead of trying to make them

Imagine if everyone who writes contracts tried to create beautiful contracts that everyone could read, understand, and use.

What if these contracts helped make negotiation easier and reduced commercial disputes?

This is a world I want to live in and it's the world I think we can create together!

There is a fun and easy way to structure a contract so you get all the legal power of a standard contract with ridiculous amounts of productivity for everyone that touches the contract (including lawyers, clients and customers).

These are what I call Reverse Sandwich Contracts.

Any intelligent fool can make things bigger, more complex and more violent. It takes a touch of genius – and a lot of courage – to move in the opposite direction

Ernst F Schumacher

What is a reverse sandwich contract?

If you are reading this book, let's assume you know what a contract is (hopefully you're not looking for sandwich recipes, because I am a pretty crappy chef). If you aren't sure or would like a refresher on contracts, head to Fitzroy Legal Service's excellent online resource The Law Handbook.

To make our contract documents and contract processes powerfully productive, we need to get the good, important stuff that often changes at the front and back and the standard stuff that doesn't change in the middle.

Ditch some of the boring bread we don't want. Get the tasty stuff out where we can see it. Now we have the good stuff on the outside – top and bottom – and a bit of bread in the middle. **A reverse sandwich!**

The very basic structure of a Reverse Sandwich Contract is:

- Key Details Table

- Terms that don't change

- Schedule/s

We want to get the good contract 'stuff' we often need to know or that often changes at the front (**Key Details Table**) and back (**Schedule**) and standardised stuff that doesn't change in the middle (**Standard Terms**).

Golden rule: If it changes regularly, pull it from the middle and put it up the front into a Key Details table or at the back into a Schedule.

We'll dive back into the intricacies and the step-by-step recipe for cooking up a Reverse Sandwich Contract soon, when we put all the secrets together.

First, I want to show you *why* we need the Reverse Sandwich Contract.

Why do we need reverse sandwich contracts?

We know we want contracts to be easy to read, negotiated fast, signed quickly, and managed more by the business, less by the legal team. Even better if the lifecycle of the document is digital and automated.

How do you structure a contract so you get all the certainty and legal punch of the traditional paper-based contracts we've come to know and tolerate with the productivity gains of digitisation and automation?

Enter the Reverse Sandwich Contract™.

A Reverse Sandwich Contract may sound silly (and messy!) but it is the crux of a proven method for making fast, usable contracts that are ready for automation.

Reverse Sandwich Contracts encourage you to think digitally about contracts, make contracts work harder for you (so you can focus your talents elsewhere) and take an active role in the contractual process.

Firstly, think of a standard sandwich.

What's going on in there? A standard sandwich doesn't let you see much of what's inside it. Same for a standard contract. (Photo credit freefoodphotos. com)

A standard sandwich has lots of boring bread on the outside and then some tasty stuff in the middle. Not terrible, but why can this be a problem for contracts?

☐ You can't always see what's inside the sandwich.

☐ There could be things in there you didn't order.

☐ You have to lift up the boring bread to see the good stuff inside.

☐ There's a lot of boring bread compared to tasty fillings.

And this is exactly what we get with a standard contract. The things which make the contract unique to each situation are hard to find and difficult to edit easily. The important terms are buried. Hidden.

With a standard contract there are:

- Ugly slabs of text that are hard to read and difficult to navigate.
- Lots of standard terms on the outside hiding the key commercial terms scattered through the contract.
- You can't always see what's inside the contract easily.
- You have to go through the entire contract to hunt for the key terms.

To make our contract documents and processes powerfully productive, resulting in a useful and useable contract, we need to get:

- the good contract stuff the contract users need to know at the front and back; and
- the standard stuff that doesn't change in the middle.

What we need to do is reverse the sandwich. Ditch some of the boring bread we don't want. Get the tasty stuff out where we can see it. Now we have the good stuff on the outside – top and bottom – and a bit of bread in the middle. A reverse sandwich!

Now don't get me wrong, the middle is extremely important. Every day, academics and practitioners are researching new and better ways to simplify and visualise the contract terms in the middle of our Reverse Contract Sandwich. **See (Triple O Productivity)** for ideas on improving the middle of the contract sandwich with plain language and visual contracting.

Before we go any further, you might be asking, 'What's so wrong with the standard contract structure? It's been working pretty well for the past few hundred plus years...'

Why change the format now?

Where there is opacity and mystification, there will be mistrust and a lack of accountability.

Richard Susskind and Daniel Susskind

Your current contract structure is slowing you down

The standard contract structure slows you down, costs you money and pisses off your customers.

The world expects speed in everything. For example, how long do you wait for a website to load before leaving?

Econsultancy found 38% of online shoppers from the UK will ditch apps and websites which don't load within 10 seconds.

Marketing specialists Portent regularly research the impact of page speed. In 2019, Portent assessed over 94 million page views across 10 e-commerce sites and found:

- 0 - 2 seconds is the ideal page load time
- Website conversion rates drop by an average of **4.42%** with each additional second of load time (between seconds 0-5)

Google loves a fast website, so if your page takes a long time to load, this can directly affect where Google ranks it in search results, and it can also indirectly affect search results with increase bounce rates.

What's harder to measure is how slow-to-read contracts affect customer experience.

There is exciting new research coming out as this book goes to print that explores the impact of contract simplification and user experience in the realm of contracts. This is an intriguing and impactful new area of research, which we can't cover in detail in this book.

We encourage interested readers to look into the work of two wonderful lawyers and researchers, Helena Haapio from Lexpert and Camilla Baasch Andersen from University of Western Australia.

Easy to read is easy to like

Caitlin Whiteman

Whey have a contract that isn't usable?

There is well-established research into processing fluency and how this powerful form of cognitive bias shapes much of what we do on a daily basis.

When you can't read a contract or use it to find information, you start to mistrust the organisation and people behind the document. This lack of trust alienates people from legal documents and processes, even though it is these very people legal documents are supposed to help!

Mistrust and confusion are not factors that lead to a great user experience. Re-reading and explaining and re-checking to confirm what was intended dramatically slows down lawyers or anyone else trying to understand a contract. Clunky, untrustworthy documents are difficult to digitize, leaving your business stuck in the past.

Useful and Useable

Standard contracts are often written by lawyers who see their job as thinking of the worst possible outcome and then protecting their clients from that terrible edge case scenario.

Standard contracts don't try to help both parties succeed or reach goals. Standard contracts aren't created for contract users.

I believe that the best, most productive contracts are contracts that are useful and useable.

These are contracts that are useful in the traditional sense of creating binding obligations and useable in the sense that they can be used by those who need to extract information from them at any point during the contract's life.

Examining the same old contract sandwich

See the below two examples of traditional, standard format contracts.

To see larger examples and analysis, head to www.createcontractsclientslove. com

Dear _____ :

This letter agreement sets forth the terms and conditions pursuant to which _____ (the "Company"), has, and will continue to engage you to provide consulting services to the Company as an independent contractor basis.

1. Services; Duties; Equipment. During the Consulting Period (as defined in Section 2 below), the Company hereby engages you to act as a _____ (e.g., social media) consultant. Your duties will include these responsibilities and other such matters as the Company may reasonably require (collectively, the "Consulting Services"). During the Consulting Period, you will: (a) render the Consulting Services as are requested from time to time by the Company in such manner as you and the Company mutually agree, including the commitment of a minimum ____ hours a week of Consulting Services; (b) render the Consulting Services ethically and conscientiously and devote your best efforts and abilities to the Company; and (c) observe all policies and directives in place from time to time by the Company for independent contractors. The Services will be non-exclusive to the Company, provided that any such other services do not interfere with or conflict with the Consulting Services to be provided by you under this letter agreement. You will also use your own equipment (including a computer) to provide the Consulting Services.

2. Consulting Period. The period during which you will provide the Consulting Services to the Company (the "Consulting Period") commences on _____ (the "Commencement Date") and will continue until _____ . This letter agreement may be terminated (i) upon _____ days written notice of termination by either party to the other, for any reason or no reason, (ii) immediately in the event of your death, disability or other incapacity resulting in your inability to perform the Consulting Services, or (iii) immediately and without written notice if you are reasonably determined by the Company to be in material breach of the terms set forth in this letter or if you commit any act or omission which involves dishonesty or disloyalty to the Company, its affiliates or any of their respective clients/customers/investors or vendors. Upon the termination of this letter agreement, the Company will have no further obligations to you under this letter agreement or otherwise, other than to make payments to you of any compensation earned on a pro-rated basis (but not yet paid) through the date of termination.

3. Compensation.

(a) In consideration of the Consulting Services provided by you under this letter agreement during the Consulting Period, you will earn consulting fees (the "Consulting Fees") in the aggregate amount of $_____ , payable in semimonthly installments.

Document is poorly formatted. "Headings" make things more confusing rather than helping to find information fast.

Difficult to see names of people or companies involved.

The type of agreement is hidden in the first paragraph, there's no agreement heading or subject line.

Key obligations (such as the number of hours of work each week) are buried among other terms.

Key information squashed together in a confusing way. It's not easy to extract the information at a glance. Here we see Consulting Period, Commencement Date and number of days notice needed to terminate are all squashed in.

Inconsistent titles and confusing language.

Why is this section called Compensation when it refers to Consulting Fees? What is "semimonthly"?

enactments of the legislation, or any legislative provision substituted for, and all legislation and regulations issued under the legislation.

e) consents, resolutions, notices and documents must be in writing and signed.

f) all actions of all of the partners must be reasonable, but unless this agreement restricts the managing partner otherwise, he or she can act as he or she thinks fit.

2. NAME, PLACE AND TERM OF BUSINESS

2.1 The name of the Partnership shall be called [insert name of business]. Its principal place of business shall be [insert business address] until changed by agreement of the Partners, but the Partnership may own property and transact business in any and all other places as may from time to time be agreed upon by the Partners.

2.2 The term of this Agreement shall be for a period of [insert number] years, commencing on [insert date], and terminating on [insert date] unless sooner terminated by mutual consent of the parties or by operation of the provisions of this Agreement.

3. PURPOSE

The purpose of the Partnership is:

3.1

3.2

3.3

4. CONFIDENTIALITY

No partner shall, during the continuance of the Partnership or for a period of [insert number] years after its termination by any means, divulge to any personnot a Partner of the Partnership any trade secret or special information employed in or conducive to the Partnership business and which may come to the Partner's knowledge in the course of this Partnership, without the consent in writing of the other Partners, or of the other Partners' heirs, administrators, or assigns.

5. CAPITAL CONTRIBUTIONS

The Partners shall each contribute [insert specified amount] cash, each, as his or her capital contribution to the Partnership. Any actual money spent prior to the ratification of this Agreement by any of the Partners shall be reimbursed from the capital contributions as soon as possible.

6. ADDITIONAL CAPITAL CONTRIBUTIONS

Whenever it is determined by the written agreement of the Partners holding a majority in capital interest of the Partnership that the Partnership's capital is or is presently likely to become insufficient for the conduct of its business, those Partners may, by written notice to all Partners, call for additional contributions to capital. These contributions shall be payable in cash no later than the date specified in the notice, or no sooner than thirty days after the notice is given. Each Partner shall be liable to the Partnership for his or her share of the aggregate contributions duly called for under this paragraph.

Headings are better, but we still have key information squashed together and difficult to find quickly. Here on page 2 of the document, business name & place of business squeezed into one sentence.

Agreement length, partnership start date & partnership end date are jammed in, making it hard to find at a glance if needed.

Another key detail is crammed into the middle of a clause, not easy to see if quickly scanning the document.

A key obligation about payment of money is tucked away in this clause.

The clause is a little uncertain around when and where to pay the money. Also what is "actual money"? I see this clause causing issues for founders....

47

These traditionally formatted contracts take a long time to negotiate, are hard to read, and are difficult to navigate when internal or external questions arise, before and after the contract is signed. This is why we reverse the contract sandwich.

What we want to do is reverse the sandwich: Pull out the ingredients from inside and ditch some of the boring bread. We're going to put the good, important stuff on the outside. Now we have good stuff on the outside — top and bottom — and a bit of bread in the middle. A reverse sandwich!

With an open sandwich, you can see what you're eating before you bite into it. The same goes for a Reverse Sandwich Contract: you can see what you are getting before you take a (contractual) bite.

Reverse sandwich contract benefits

When you Reverse Sandwich a contract, you get a contract that is:

- more 'hands off' from the legal team
- useful and usable for lawyers and non-lawyers
- easier to manage and control
- ready for electronic signatures
- not filled with unnecessary terms, pages or process steps
- client-friendly
- optimised for automated workflows
- ready for paperless offices
- a delight to read
- easy to sign
- stress-free to manage
- fast to navigate
- simple to vary later
- painless to adjust for different parties
- futuristic and sexy!

So, when we put all these awesome attributes together, what do we end up with? What does a productive contract look like?

What does a reversed contract look like?

What does our Reverse Sandwich Contract look?

Here's look at a basic agreement after the Reverse Sandwich treatment.

To see larger examples and analysis,
head to www.createcontractsclientslove.com.

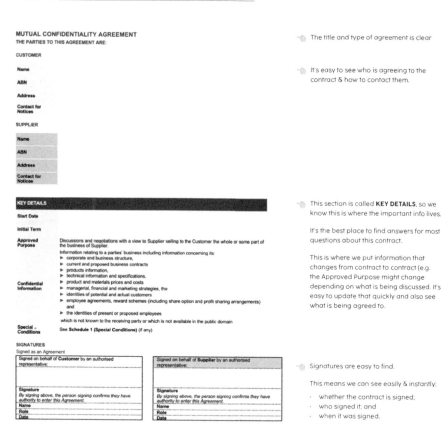

MUTUAL CONFIDENTIALITY AGREEMENT
THE PARTIES TO THIS AGREEMENT ARE:

CUSTOMER

Name

ABN

Address

Contact for Notices

SUPPLIER

Name

ABN

Address

Contact for Notices

KEY DETAILS

Start Date

Initial Term

Approved Purpose — Discussions and negotiations with a view to Supplier selling to the Customer the whole or some part of the business of Supplier.

Information relating to a parties' business including information concerning its:
- corporate and business structure,
- current and proposed business contracts
- products information,
- technical information and specifications,
- product and materials prices and costs
Confidential Information — managerial, financial and marketing strategies, the
- identities of potential and actual customers
- employee agreements, reward schemes (including share option and profit sharing arrangements) and
- the identities of present or proposed employees

which is not known to the receiving party or which is not available in the public domain

Special Conditions — See **Schedule 1 (Special Conditions)** (if any)

SIGNATURES
Signed as an Agreement

Signed on behalf of **Customer** by an authorised representative:	Signed on behalf of **Supplier** by an authorised representative:
Signature	Signature
By signing above, the person signing confirms they have authority to enter this Agreement.	By signing above, the person signing confirms they have authority to enter this Agreement.
Name	Name
Role	Role
Date	Date

The title and type of agreement is clear

It's easy to see who is agreeing to the contract & how to contact them.

This section is called **KEY DETAILS**, so we know this is where the important info lives.

It's the best place to find answers for most questions about this contract.

This is where we put information that changes from contract to contract (e.g. the Approved Purpose might change depending on what is being discussed. It's easy to update that quickly and also see what is being agreed to.

Signatures are easy to find.

This means we can see easily & instantly:
· whether the contract is signed;
· who signed it; and
· when it was signed.

BACKGROUND

A. Supplier and Customer propose to enter into discussions and negotiations for the Approved Purpose.

B. In the course of this activity, each party may disclose to the other Confidential Information.

C. The parties intend each of them will at all times throughout any discussions maintain the confidentiality of the Confidential Information for the purposes of protecting their respective interests in the Confidential Information and to advance the prospect of them concluding a mutually satisfactory commercial agreement contemplated by these recitals.

IT IS AGREED

Full agreement

1. This Agreement outlines the full agreement between the parties and any amendment of this Agreement must be in writing and signed by the parties

Definitions

2. Unless the context requires otherwise:
   a. capitalised terms in this Agreement have the meaning given to them in the Key Details table at the front of this Agreement; and
   b. words which are defined in the Privacy Act 1988 mean the same thing in this Agreement.

Keep confidential

3. Each party must keep Confidential Information confidential and must not disclose it or make it available directly or indirectly to any third party in any form or medium whatsoever without the express written consent of the owner of the relevant Confidential Information.

Commercially sensitive

4. Each party acknowledges that the Confidential Information is commercially sensitive and valuable and that any unauthorised disclosure or use of it could give rise to considerable damage.

Approved Purpose only

5. The Parties agree not to use or exploit the other party's Confidential Information for any purpose other than the Approved Purpose without express written consent.

Agents to keep confidential

6. Neither party may permit any employee, agent or subcontractor of that party to have access to the Confidential Information until that employee, agent or subcontractor has signed a confidentiality agreement with the disclosing party in a form approved by the other party.

Notice of disclosure

7. Each party must immediately notify the other party of any information, which comes to its attention regarding any actual or potential unauthorized disclosure or use of the Confidential Information. Each party must co-operate with the other in any investigation, prosecution, litigation or other action taken regarding the subject of any such information.

Injunction

8. In the event of any actual or alleged unauthorised disclosure of use of Confidential Information by any future, existing or former employee, agent or subcontractor of a party, that party must enforce its rights to injunctive or other relief to the fullest extent possible or, if requested by the other party, assign such rights to the other party. Each party must reasonably assist the other party in enforcing those rights.

Termination or expiry

9. Upon termination or completion of discussions, each party must deliver to the other all Confidential Information in their possession or control. Each party must delete or destroy any Confidential Information contained in any computer memory or other recording media in its possession or control which is not capable of delivery.

Here are our standard terms.

These generally don't change.

If these terms do change or have been negotiated, we can use a Special Conditions schedule at the back of the document.

Clauses have clear headings. If we do need to find information here within the middle of the agreement, we can find it quickly.

See the difference?

Which format would you rather use to locate information?

Which agreement is faster to negotiate?

Now we have a simplified contract, we can start exploring ways to make it even faster.

An extra pair of (robotic) legal hands

When I first started using electronic signatures in software platforms to form electronic contracts (i.e. contracts that are signed electronically), I was ecstatic just to be rid of the life force drain that is having piles of paper contracts lying around.

Not to mention the pain of scanning documents in ... chasing signatures ... mailing things out ... Urgh. What a nightmare! Especially when you start to realise it is completely unnecessary work that takes hours to do something that should take minutes.

Then, I began testing out more application features to build further productivity into the contracts with automated contract workflows. This is when I saw the real power of these applications.

With these applications, I could outsource myself in a way to extend the legal team with virtual, automated assistance.

It was like the legal team could now be everywhere! We had considerable oversight and could fix things rapidly. Legal was no longer the bottleneck of the business. We had released the 'Handbrake to Happiness'. The BPU (Business Prevention Unit) was no more!

When you start to think of automation tools as your team mates, then you can really create a huge impact on your own productivity and help more people, faster.

Targeted automation means you can outsource your own smarts to extend your legal team.

Go low tech to start

Reverse Sandwich Contracting™ is certainly not the only way to structure and automate paperless contracts. If you want useability, speed, and overall control, this method beats out far more expensive, software or AI driven options.

Reverse Sandwich Contracting™ methods are translatable onto other word processing, document assembly, automation, and electronic signature platforms.

I generally use Microsoft Word and whatever platform my clients use. If you can find a few hours and you have Google Docs or Microsoft Word (and of course this book!), you are well on the way to creating a well-designed and cleverly automated contract.

Before we roll up our sleeves and start cooking up a reverse sandwich contract, we need to re-train the way we look at contracts. We need to see contracts for what they are (and what they could become).

A CONTRACT IS NOT A BIT OF PAPER

MINDSET:
Think digitally

A rolling contract gathers no moss

A contract is not just a bit of paper, signed and forgotten, only to be remembered when there's a problem.

A contract can be like sheets of music for an orchestra. It can direct each musician how to play their instrument, what style to play in, when to play and how long to play for. The composer might not have expertise to play all the instruments, but they have an idea of how it will all come together.

How can those composing and drafting contracts make beautiful contract music that is easy to understand and easy to play?

When your contract is on song, all the musicians – those involved in doing the work within the contract – are playing together and making amazing music. When your contract and contract process are out of whack, your musicians aren't in sync with each other.

There are notes going everywhere. The drum is beating out of time. The high notes sound shrill without the balancing lower notes of harmony. And everyone feels stressed because they think they are reading the music correctly, that it's everyone else who has it wrong. This is where many contracts end up.

How can contract composers and conductors make contracts easy to understand? Can a contract make a contractual process smoother? Can a contract increase the positive relationship between contracting parties?

We need to stop seeing a contract as a bit of paper. It's not just a bit of paper. A contract is ultimately a map to guide a relationship between people.

A contract is ultimately a map to guide the relationship between people.

Even when it's a company that signs on the dotted line, in the end it's people who must carry out the obligations in a contract.

What does this mean? It means that you cannot look at a contract in isolation from the process that it sits within. You must look to understand what the people involved want to get out of the contract. Find out what the contract has done before. Importantly, you need to know the actual steps people will take once they have a document ready to sign. **In Secret 9**, we go deeper into making the people driven contract process productive.

Because your contract involves people and processes, you must understand both. The drafting of a contract and understanding the contract lifecycle go hand in hand.

We need to stop seeing a contract as a bit of paper.
It's not a just bit of paper.

Your contract involves people and processes – you must understand both.

What can fall away...?

When you start thinking digitally, paper-based contracts and paper-based processes show their true nature.

It's like comparing old home phones to smart phones. Paper contracts and traditionally formatted documents start to look like old daggy brick phones. They feel slow, heavy, and even ridiculous. Digitally optimised contracts are sexier and faster.

As you think digitally and work your way through this book, you'll start to see things in a new light and ask questions you didn't ask before. Are there unnecessary approvals we could streamline? Does it go to the customer first when it needs management sign off? Should the finance team get a heads-up when it is finished so they can start creating a customer account?

These questions and more will often answer themselves as you run through the rest of the contract productivity secrets towards reverse sandwiching your contract.

Contracts are not just for lawyers. Most contracts are used by operational and customer service teams to solve problems people encounter every day. The issue is, they are relying on documents other than the contract to solve those problems. Only the lawyer understands the contract. Some follow 'business rules' instead of the contract, or the statement of work which sits outside the contract, or the handshake deal that is the opposite to the contract.

Then, we have unclear objectives, confused delivery schedules, basic 'legal' questions which aren't really legal (such as when is the start date of the contract, when do I have to provide the service, when can I terminate, what products can I promote, ... etc.).

Most of these problems and basic questions are solved if the contract itself is readable and user-friendly. Even where a problem is not fully solved, contract users can ask more informed questions of their legal advisors.

The legal advisors have fewer admin-related questions. Fewer disputes arise with a contract that is easy to understand now, and in the future when it's picked up by someone outside of the deal.

It's just easier, fairer, and faster to think digitally from the start and make your contract usable in the reality of our digital business culture.

Contracts are undergoing fundamental changes.

New technology and new design are transforming the look and feel of contracts, and entirely new contract genres are being born.

Helena Haapio, Daniela Alina Plewe, and Robert deRooy

Thinking digitally

A contract today needs to be more than just a paper document. So we must stop thinking in terms of one sided pieces of A4 paper (or whatever that odd 'letter' size is which our lovely American friends use)·

We need to think about what contracts do and what we want them to do. We need to think about contracts digitally. Maybe you already do think digitally. Perfect! You can encourage others and build a digital culture in your organisation.

Digital and digitisation continue to be buzzwords in the corporate jargon swag bag. But what do they mean? And how can we 'go digital' and embrace digitisation?

Karel Dörner and David Edelman from global management consulting firm McKinsey and Company outlined the three key aspects of thinking digitally.

Thinking digitally means you are:

- Creating value at the new frontiers of the business world; and

- Creating value in the processes that execute a vision of customer experiences; and

- Building foundational capabilities that support the entire structure.

Imagine if we brought these concepts to the table every time we approach a new contract? Thinking digitally becomes less of a buzzword, '...less as a thing [in itself] and more a way of doing things.'

Creating digital, automation-ready contracts is just how you do things.

Once you start thinking digitally and approaching your day-to-day work with a digital mindset, you start to notice the things that don't perform in a digital world. When you're thinking digitally, things that reduce productivity stick out like dog poo on white carpet.

Think about the world a contract lives in today.

When we want to send someone a copy of a contract, we don't photocopy it and bind it and post it anymore. We scan it in and send the contracts as a PDF via email. You don't just sell or buy products from within your own city, you deal with people around the world and sign contracts with international companies.

When disputes happen, we don't need to look through a meticulously tabbed contract folder to find the right clauses. Just as you can now search quickly and easily for everything your heart desires online, you can search digital documents easily and even use text recognition tools on scanned documents.

We don't need to carefully alphabetise our contract filing system and keep all variations together, we simply name our files and folders or use metadata (like Date Modified) to find what we are looking for.

Paper is an unnecessary step for most contracts in the digital world.

Build an extraordinary skill set

There's never been a worse time to be a worker with only 'ordinary' skills... digital technologies are acquiring these skills... at an extraordinary rate.

Erik Brynjolfsson and Andrew McAfee

As Erik Brynjolfsson and Andrew McAfee point out in their excellent book The Second Machine Age, if you have only 'ordinary' skills, you'll be left behind. Embracing new ways of working and looking at work digitally is an amazing way to build an extraordinary skillset. Take the time to learn new digital skills and think about your work in the digital context.

A contract is a digital tool with the power to enhance your personal and professional speed, accuracy, and experience. Start exploring what it means for a contract to be a contract in our digital world.

Once you do that, your productivity naturally increases as you notice unnecessary things and start to get rid of them. As you move through this book, remember to keep thinking digitally. Think of your audience. Think of who uses your contracts.

Think about ways your digital contract can best serve its users in a digital world and provide a guidepost for them in the contract relationship.

A contract can be a digital tool with the power to enhance your personal and professional productivity.

BE A LAZY LAWYER

MINDSET:
Delegate like a diva

When I have a tough job ...and can't find an easy way to do it, I have a lazy man put on it. He'll find an easy way to do it ....

Clarence E. Bleicher

How many hours do you have in your day?

People often quote that we all have the same number of hours in the day as Beyoncé, Barack Obama, Richard Branson, and every other celebrity. Not sure about you but I don't always find this super motivating when they are all extremely rich and I'm trying to cut down on buying coffee when I'm out to save cash to afford a house deposit.

But break the concept down past the money, fame ... and talent.

I think a key reason celebrities can get so much done is they are extremely good at outsourcing. Whether you want to call it delegation, subcontracting, automation, or reallocation, all these terms really mean someone (or something) other than you is doing the work.

Who can you get to do your work so you can increase your productivity to A-list celebrity levels?

Why, minions of course...

Minions

The term 'minion' has come to have insulting, even derogatory meaning today. From the depiction of minion henchmen as real but rather stupid people to minions as quirky, yellow, loveable aliens, if you get called a minion, it's unlikely you'd be happy about it.

It wasn't always the case.

The word 'minion' comes from the French term 'mignon'. Back in the (French) day, the term 'minion' meant 'darling'. It was used to describe a person who the king or queen particularly liked. A 'minion' was an important person's favourite follower. Then, the term 'mignon' changed to express something as 'dainty' or 'delicate'. You might be familiar with the *filet mignon* cut of meat.

Only later did the term change to mean something more offensive or insulting.

Why the linguistics discussion?

I don't want you to think I am being harsh when I say to look out for minions. It isn't intended to be a put-down or insult to inexperienced, junior level workers. It's just a fact of life. Some people are well placed to help you out with routine and repetitive tasks. Some people should be your minions and do your (reasonable, never evil) bidding.

Minions come in all shapes and sizes and seniority levels in a workplace. And when you learn to delegate like a diva, you will start to see minions pop up everywhere who can help you (and your contracts!) explode with productivity.

Find the right minion for the job and you are well on your way to productivity gains for yourself and your company. You can even have those senior to you unwittingly become a minion when you start delegating like a celebrity.

But what kind of minions should you be looking out for?

I'm glad you asked. There are several different types:

- Minion Minions
- Robot Minions
- Contract Owner Minions
- Other Party Minions

Some people are happy to be your minion and do your (reasonable, never evil) bidding.

Minion Minions

Minions might be a work experience person, a paralegal, an assistant, a junior lawyer, a student keen to learn, or sometimes a person you manage. Finding minions is very valuable. Not just for you, but often for the minion also. Minions are generally very happy to help out. This is especially the case where you explain how useful the task is for the greater good and how they can learn about exciting things happening in their area of interest.

There are big benefits for the minion also! For a minion, the opportunity to help with your drudgery might be exciting. Working on larger matters or with different people is a way for minions to reduce their own drudgery. The opportunity to add a new feather to their skillset bow can also be enticing for minions.

When I started out as a paralegal, I needed to take care of paper filing systems. This meant scanning in stacks of contracts, reading them and working out what they were about, creating a little paper file tab, entering them into the spreadsheet (our electronic filing system at the time) and physically filing them away.

I was a minion, and I was happy to be one!

Sure, it wasn't an amazingly exciting task, but it gave me an excellent overview of the business, of new and different types of contracts. My time as a minion convinced me paper was dead, inspired me to innovate and pushed me to find ways to get things done more efficiently – and here we are! My time as a minion convinced me paper was dead, inspired me to innovate and pushed me to find ways to get things done more efficiently -- and here we are!

So, the moral here is don't feel bad about delegating tasks. Sometimes minions might be interested in it, sometimes they might just have to do it because it's their job. If you're nice about asking, give full information on how to do the task well and let them know you're open to their input on how to optimise the task, there is nothing wrong with delegating work to others.

Keep your eyes out for minions. If someone offers to help, let them! And follow them up on it. Find them something to do – tasks such as basic knowledge management work i.e. 'watch me and write down all the steps I do' or the pre-work to map out a process or the actual tasks you don't want to do anymore.

Robot Minions

Robot Minions aren't actual, humanoid robots with 'arms' and robo-wheels (unless you have one in which case, cool, can I borrow?). When I talk about using robot minions, I mean automated and digital tools. For the purposes of this book, I am mainly referring to low-code robot minions.

High-tech legal tools and software are amazing, but they require big budgets and lots of time. When I speak about robot minions in this book, we'll be referring to some basic robot minions you can easily create and manage.

Software as an Expensive Service

There are lots of electronic contract and electronic signature applications which promise to create you an amazing contract with a few simple clicks. I have tested lots of them out. Some of them some have the potential to be amazing. However, the development time to create them, the cost to buy licences and set up, the cost to create a customised set of questions (just for one contract!), the huge time needed to explain your business processes to another company, the testing of a solution etc etc... It gets exhausting, with little progress to show for time invested.

Increasing contract productivity with automation requires testing and tweaking. This testing and tweaking can quickly escalate costs if you go to an external party who doesn't understand your business. Even more so if you don't understand your business processes yourself. Often the external party controls the passwords and content, so every change means you need to dig into your (already limited) legal budget.

It was all just too slow and too expensive. I didn't have the budget in our tiny team to put into one type of document.

Don't get me wrong, I love what these applications can do. The advances made in automation, intelligent analysis and other futuristic legal tech tools are incredible. But there are a few issues with mega-tech.

Main issues with silver bullet SaaS

There are four main issues with SaaS (Software as a Service) or any software applications that promise to 'solve it all':

1. The pricing of the technology puts it out of reach of most but the largest of legal teams and firms.

2. The time needed to 'teach' a robot (and its robot handlers) about one contract is considerable.

3. This type of software often tries to put robot lipstick on a pig of a contract – the contract itself is confusing and difficult to read (not to mention the backend contract creation processes and ongoing lifecycle).

4. There's no silver bullet SaaS – nothing will fix all of your contracting problems or grant all of your contracting wishes.

Some software promises a cure-all but often tries to put robot lipstick on a pig of a contract

If you have your contract and process at perfect productivity levels (see **Triple O Productivity**), have a good amount of time, quite a bit of money, and you can also accurately provide a set of requirements to the software provider, then you might see a good return on the investment of cash and effort.

If you're not quite there yet, read on!

The designa dn automation tactics in this book work well with low-code solutions to help frame your contracts and get ready for high-code solutions down the track. If you don't have a $100k+ legal tech budget or weeks to set aside to workshop your contract with external consultants and you truly want to create beautiful, fair, fast, productive contracts, then Reverse Sandwich Contracting™ is for you.

The automated workflow

One of my favourite robot minions is the automated workflow. Simple examples of automated workflows include:

Automatic email responses

So basic, so easy! Get your email working harder for you to point in the direction of your FAQs or other resources you've already built. This works excellently for team mailboxes e.g. legal@smallcorporate.com and allows you to inject personality into the legal team rather than a boring canned response.

See **createcontractsclientslove.com** for more ideas on sneaky hidden pre-filled email links and triage tables to use to gather better instructions from clients.

Electronic signature platform templates

Most eSignature platforms have a template or workflow feature which allows you to set up a standard structure to guide the creation of a signed contract. See for example DocuSign's guide on setting up a template. These automated workflows allow you to set up a document you use often and then easily apply the same fields and signature tabs again and again to different documents. You can then step it up a notch (with a little extra cash for upgraded features) and test out added features on these platforms, such as PowerForms.

Low-code document assembly

Want to create a low-code way for clients or customers to pre-populate information directly into a template contract? Easy! Use Google Forms and the Form Publisher extension and you're good to go! In the same vein, you could have clients enter information into a spreadsheet which you then mail merge with a pre-templated document. A little fiddly (and less robot-y) but still gets someone else doing the admin.

Integrators (low-code)

What if you got a special notification every time your boss sent you an email. Perhaps you want to text your husband automatically when you leave work to say you're on your way. A reminder to take an umbrella when rain is forecast. IFTTT (If this then that), Zapier, and Microsoft Flows are just some of many applications which automatically do something if something else happens.

For contract purposes, these alerts can:

- let you know when a Google Forms survey is complete

- tell you a document was added into a certain folder

- link up two separate applications

There's lots of playing and fiddling to find out new ways to connect applications usefully so the human effort (and error!) is taken out.

APIs (Application Programming Interfaces)

Integrations between different application systems like SalesForce and HelloSign can automatically extract customer info and prepopulate a contract with it. Or your webform can link in with the Australian Business Register to search and confirm Australian Business Numbers – no more missed digits and typos! Whilst they require greater coding skills, they can make your life easier. Ask a friendly IT person if there are integrations available for your company's customer relationship management system.

Robot minions are here to stay

There's not time to go into all software options in this book, however it is important to keep an open mind to new technology as it arises.

And, if you meet any robo-sceptics, just point them towards the seven stages of robot replacement below...

Seven Stages of Robot Replacement

What stage are you at in Kevin Kelly's *seven stages of robot replacement*?

1. A robot or computer cannot possibly do the tasks I do!

Later....

2. OK, it can do a lot of them, but it can't do everything I do.

Later....

3. OK, it can do everything I do, except it needs me when it breaks down, which is often.

Later....

4. OK, it operates flawlessly on routine stuff, but I need to train it for new tasks.

Later....

5. OK, it can have my old boring job, it's obvious that was not a job humans were meant to do.

Later....

6. Wow, now robots are doing my old job, my new job is much more fun and pays more!

Later...

7. I am so glad a robot/computer cannot possibly do what I do now.

Contract owner minions

The person asking you to create or help with a contract (a.k.a. the Contract Owner) is a perfect minion. The Contract Owner Minion often is a salesperson, a manager, or a HR person. The Contract Owner has the most skin in the game and is generally the keenest to get a contract finalised fast. This means you can harness the Contract Owner's keenness into contract admin action.

The person who asked you for the contract is generally the one most keen to see it signed. It's their sales commission or their new hire or their supply agreement, so they have both the urgency to get the contract document completed as well as information required in the contract.

Depending on their level of seniority and the information they have, push certain admin tasks out to the Contract Owner to complete. This is efficient. They will often need to give you information for the contract anyway. Instead of getting this information in dribs and drabs via email, you make it clear what information must be provided and where.

What does this look like? At a very basic level, this could mean you provide the HR officer with a locked-down template document with form fields for them to fill out.

As outlined above in the *Robot Minions* section, to step up a level, a salesperson could put customer information and purchase detail into a spreadsheet (or a survey in Google Forms, which builds a spreadsheet #lowcode) that you then mail merge into a pre-prepared contract template.

When you start exploring digital document creation via DocuSign or other electronic signature platforms with automated workflows, you can assign certain parts of the contract document for others to fill out. Each person automatically receives an email with a link to the document, fills out what they need to and approves for the next person in the line. Then you just check over their work at the end (with the power to reject or pause for questions if there are issues).

These low-code, simple solutions keep your template documents secure at the same time as pushing low-value work out to those most keen to complete it.

You can harness the Contract Owner's keenness into productive contract action... and get work off your to do list.

Other party minion

Getting customers or suppliers to enter their own information into documents is somewhat controversial depending on how you want to structure your customers' experience.

We are used to entering information and form filling, so it might not be as offensive to ask the other party to enter their details. Where the other side enters their own information, or selects options, it saves you time and drudgery. Let's face it, they will do it quicker than you anyway.

However, I can understand if you want to keep customers out of the drudgery of admin.

Last stop – what if you have no minions?

What if you can't find a minion, you don't like doing a task and you aren't adding value?

If you've seen The Princess Bride, you might remember the scenes in 'The Pit of Despair'. The hero character 'Westley' is captured by villains who restrain him onto a table, place metal suction cups onto each of his temples, and then a machine (creatively called 'The Machine') proceeds to suck the life out of our handsome hero.

When you are doing work that you don't like and you aren't adding value, it can feel like life is getting sucked out of you. You become frustrated, bored, and irritated. Perhaps it's a bit melodramatic, but if you are stuck doing this kind of drudgery work, sometimes it feels like you're stuck in The Pit of Despair.

If you dislike a contract-related task and aren't adding much value, it is the pits.

What to do when you're in the contractual Pit of Despair

Is written to help guide you through different steps to get you out of the Pit of Despair caused by contract task drudgery.

1. Are being you active or creative enough in looking for and finding Robot Minions, Contract Owner Minions, Customer Minions or run-of-the-mill minions to do that task? Re-read this section.

2. It's likely you haven't made the contract task fully productive yet — **see Triple O Productivity.**

3. Discuss the task with others in your team and people who use the contract (or contact the author) to see if anyone has tackled something similar.

If you still really must do the horrible task, there are two productive steps you can take.

☐   Make it as fun as possible; and

☐   Track your metrics.

Make it fun

Put some good music on whilst you do that hated task. Get a massage when it's finished. Have a nice cup of tea whilst you're doing it. Fix the font.

Whatever you could do to make it less annoying, do it. There's interesting research on '*Temptation Bundling*' by Katherine Milkman which shows you're more likely to do an undesirable task (such as exercise) when you bundle it with something you perceive as fun (such as listening to a good audiobook).

Favourite music playlist on at work whilst completing contract admin? Yes please!

Pedicure whilst completing contract management admin? Why not!

Batch responding to overdue work emails with a dirty chai latte at your favourite café? Productivity bonus round!

Track your metrics

Make it a challenge to finish the dreaded task as quickly as possible each time.

- Time yourself.
- Track your progress.
- Get better at finishing it quickly.
- Map out the exact steps you take to get the task done accurately and fast.

Then you're ready to start training someone up as a minion or research potential robot minions. By tracking and measuring you might start to notice ways to systemise the painful task. When a minion appears, you'll be ready!

Ready to see a diva's systematised approach to delegation?

How to delegate like a diva

Whilst Beyoncé probably doesn't use this exact list when she delegates important tasks (perhaps she's even delegated her delegations?), there is a helpful outsourcing order to ensure maximum productivity.

Think of daily tasks you need to get done. It's easy to think of tasks you dislike doing or which are admin heavy to start with. Run through the below list of questions and see if you can spot areas for improvement.

Note: Steps 1 and 2 below are about **Obliterating** and **Optimising** your contract document and contract process. We'll learn more about these concepts in the next section, Triple O Productivity.

The 'delegate like a diva' checklist

1. Does it really need to be done?

Yes? ↓ Continue ... if No... just stop doing it! Huzzah!

2. Is this the best way to do this task?

Yes? ↓ Continue... if No... time to develop the best way to do that task, see Triple O productivity section for more!

3. Robot Minion: Is there a robot or automated way to get this done?

No? ↓ Continue... If yes, document new process and relax!

4. Contract Owner Minion: Can the person who asked me to create this contract do that for me?

No? ↓ Continue... If yes, document new process and relax!

5. Other Party Minion: Can the other person signing the contract do that for me?

No? ↓ Continue... If yes, document new process and relax!

6. Minion Minion: Can a 'minion' do that for me (with some training and patience)?

No? ↓ Continue... If yes, document new process then train and supervise minion.

7. Value & Enjoyment: Am I adding value if I do that or do I like doing it?

No? ↓ Continue... If yes, document the process and keep adding value!

8. Uh oh, looks like you are in the Pit of Despair....

- ☐ Map out the exact steps you take to get the task done accurately and fast.
- ☐ Time yourself doing the task and track your progress over time.
- ☐ Research future tech upgrades that could take this task off your hands.
- ☐ See the Checklist Legal website for how to build a business case for innovation.

Be a lazy lawyer
Delegate like a diva

TRIPLE O PRODUCTIVITY

MINDSET:
Systematise productivity hacking

Are you ready for organised chaos?

So far, we've learnt three of the four key tactics to *Create and Automate Better Contracts*. We are starting to apply these secrets on our journey to making contracts productive.

Let's do a quick recap before diving into the fourth tactic, Triple O Productivity.

We know we can't keep making the same old boring contract sandwich. We first learnt to think about structuring for speed. We need to think about structuring our contracts like a Reverse Sandwich — with good stuff that changes on the outside and standard stuff that stays the same on the inside. We're on the lookout for things that change and key details so we can get them closer together to make life easier and faster.

We understand from tactic two that our contract is not a piece of paper, it's a map to the relationship between real people in a real world. We are thinking digitally about our contract and being open to changing the contract to work better in a digital culture.

Not all of us have the luxury of skilled, intelligent assistants. Never mind! When you start thinking like a lazy (but productive!) lawyer like we heard from tactic three, we know we will start to see different minions (robot and human) who can help with the work where we aren't adding value.

With those three tactics in mind, it's time for tactic four on our road to designing amazing contracts. It's time to get your hands dirty in your contract document and your contract process, with *Triple O Productivity*.

Productivity inspired by a classic system

I first fell in love with formal productivity hacking systems when I first read David Allen's Getting Things Done book. The book details a productivity system for 'stress-free productivity' which is affectionately known as GTD by Allen's keen tribe of followers. Celebrity GTD fans include Daniel Pink (author of Drive), Jeff Boliba (VP of Burton Snowboards) and many other non-famous, everyday folks (like me!).

The GTD system method involves many great ideas such as creating an external 'brain' to keep your own clear and the Weekly Review. I know when I am getting angsty or feeling overwhelmed at work, it's usually because I've skipped the Weekly Review. The GTD system now even has science behind it on top of the raving fans.

Reworked versions of the GTD system and the ongoing spins each person puts on GTD for themselves are intriguing. Many developers, founders, and engineers have used Allen's tried and true system to build apps and productivity systems such as:

- Michael Sliwinski, CEO and founder of Nozbe, was heavily influenced by GTD in building the Nozbe mobile and desktop app (an app that I love!);

- Ari Meisel who, amongst other life hacks, takes a logical approach to David Allen's work;

- The Productivity Show, a podcast by the team at Asian Efficiency, regularly promotes the GTD system;

- Not to mention a quick search in Amazon for GTD reveals various add on guides and lessons.

Taking my interest in personal productivity hacking and interest in quantifying practically everything, I developed a systematic approach for nudging contract documents and contract processes towards powerful productivity, in preparation of digital processes. That process is Triple O Productivity.

What is Triple O Productivity?

Triple O Productivity is a way to structure your thinking if a contract document or contract process is causing stress, increasing anxiety or slowing you down.

Maybe you aren't stressed but you are keen to stay at peak productivity and want to build more productivity into each area of your business. Contracts are an excellent area to start with.

Triple O Productivity is Secret Four and it works to make contract documents and contract processes more productive in three different ways with the three 'O's of productivity: Obliterate, Optimise & Outsource

Obliterate the parts of your contract document and contract process that cause issues or slow you down.

Optimise the essential parts of the document and process. Now all information is clear and easy to read, the process flows smoothly and the key details can be found when needed.

Outsource as much of the drudgery (i.e. repetitive, admin-heavy tasks) as you can, preferably to a robot of some description or to key users of the contract.

We'll apply the Triple O Productivity approach to the contract document and also to the contract process. Triple O Productivity is an ongoing method to put into action when something just isn't working.

Sometimes when you've streamlined the process, it might make sense to adjust the document, or vice versa. You may want to repeat these steps over the process or document again at regular intervals to ensure you are keeping your productivity gains at their maximum.

If organizations actively monitored the extent of value lost through poor contracting, they would become relentless in the push for change.

World Commerce and Contracting

Should I start with the Contract or the Process?

Good question; you are very clever! It's a difficult one to answer and honestly, I am not sure there is one right way. Personally, I start with the contract document. I do this for a few reasons:

As a lawyer, I often have easy access to the contract and generally people will believe me if I say I can make (good) changes to the contract. Although this can vary widely depending on how protective people are of their precedents in your organisation or firm.

From reading the contract, I get a general idea of what might change often, what the process is supposed to be and where information needs to come from. You can't really build a process map without reading the contract document, so I start by reviewing the contract document for productivity gains I can make from redesigning the project.

We can make quick wins with the contract document (see the *Quick Contract Wins* checklist in the **Resources** section). With these quick wins, you'll see some gains straightaway. Little wins lead to big wins.

As you get more skilled in contract design, there are some basic information design techniques to improve basic contracts before you even know everything about the process and the purpose.

Processes involving other people can be harder to change. If you have evidence of your idea with a partially redesigned document, people are more likely to listen to you when you suggest changes to the contract process.

When is it a good idea to start with the contract process first instead of the contract document?

- ☐ When it's not your contract
- ☐ When the process isn't working at all or is the main issue
- ☐ When there is a change of people or decision makers, so it's a good time to change the process.

I've included thought provoking questions for you at each step of the Triple O Productivity method, for both the contract document and the contract process. These questions aim to get your mind thinking of different possibilities relevant for your contract circumstances.

The questions are not exhaustive and are not a complete checklist to follow. You may develop your own sets of questions tailored for the way you and your business or firm think about productivity and the unique challenges in your industry.

Key questions are formatted as below. They frame the way to approach the contract document or contract process when applying each step of the Triple O Productivity method.

Key questions: There's a key question to approach the review with and then several other Firestarter questions to help you think digitally about your contract documents and process.

Ready? Before you start obliterating, there are some key tactics to keep in mind …

Before you begin

There are a few key things to remember before you start ripping into your contract document.

Save a copy of the old version

Keep a copy of the old version somewhere safe; you might need it again for reference or to compare to later.

Get some metrics

Gather some rough numbers and other data around the old contract such as:

- How long does it take you to prepare a contract each time?

- How many times per month would you complete a contract?

- How many words and/or pages are in the old version?

- What is the average turnaround time from initial request for a contract to fully signed agreement?

- How many disputes involve this contract?

You can set up a basic quiz (use Google Forms or Survey Monkey etc) to ask users what they think of the contract document and contract process. Ask your internal clients and ask customers if possible. You could time how long it takes people to find information in the contract and then run a test with the old and the new versions to assess time saved.

This can help show to yourself and others the value of making contracts more productive. For example, to explain to your manager a process that used to take one month now takes two days is extremely valuable.

See www.createcontractsclientslove.com for more resources and spreadsheets on developing metrics to support your contract design projects and innovation business case.

Track your changes

You may want to keep a record of the changes you've made. You can work with track changes on,[44] or use the compare documents feature when you're done. Either way, it is important to remember what's changed from the earlier version.

PRODUCTIVE CONTRACT DOCUMENT

MINDSET:
Design for readability

A readable contract is a likeable contract.

A likable contract is a productive contract. A productive contract is a profitable contract.

If you focus on making your contracts readable, you are focusing on making them more profitable for the company.

Time to go to simplification town...

Now that we're thinking digitally and ready to structure our contract so it is useful and usable, it's time to go to town on the document content. Applying Triple O Productivity is fun! There's nothing as satisfying as cutting an entire unnecessary clause or rewording legalese.

I love the way a freshly created Key Details table can cut the clutter of a contract, and soon you will too! You don't have to be a lawyer to write a contract, but it's a good idea to have a lawyer check over your work if you aren't a lawyer (doesn't have to be me!).

Easy to read is easy to like

Caitlin Whiteman

Obliterate (Contract Document)

>>Key Question: Does this part of the contract help support the main purpose of the contract?

There's no point optimising or outsourcing a contract that's filled with unnecessary information. Our first step is to Obliterate parts of our contract document that we don't need.

We're on the lookout for terms that change to structure our document for usability and because we're thinking digitally, we'll start to notice the things we can shed. To jumpstart the Obliterate step, head to the *Quick Wins Checklist* and start deleting with delight!

Review the contract document and ask yourself, **does this part of the contract help support the purpose of the contract?**

More information is not necessarily good information

Cushla Schofield

Other questions to consider:

☐   What is the true purpose of that part of the contract?

☐   Do we need that part of the document at all?

☐   Does that part of the contract matter?

☐   When is that part ever used?

☐   What areas of the document are no longer in line with actual processes?

☐   Why is that part repeated?

Optimise (Contract Document)

>>Key Questions: What changes in this contract and what stays the same? Is there a way to make this part of the contract clearer?

This is where we get down to business and make the Reverse Sandwich Contract come to life. This is clearly my favourite part. It can take a little time but it's well worth it. Once the unnecessary things are out of the contract, we're now going to optimise what's left.

To get into the full concept of the Reverse Sandwich Contract™ structure, see the *Putting it all together* section where the step-by-step process is included.

If you aren't sure what to pull up to the front and what to push to a schedule, check out the guidelines here on Key Details Tables and Schedules.

At this step, we are looking to get the very best out of our contract. We are structuring the contract like a Reverse Sandwich. We are formatting the document to look good. We are keeping our lazy lawyer mind switched on to find ways to automate or outsource document creation wherever possible. We use plain language so every clause will shine and sparkle with clarity.

We think of engaging ways to present dense information such as flow charts, tables and pictures. We are SLAPPing the contract into shape (see **below**).

The key questions we are asking here are 'What changes in this contract and what stays the same?' and 'Is there a way to make this part of the contract clearer?'

Other questions to ask when reviewing the contract document for potential optimisation:

- Are all the clauses and key details structured in a way that makes sense?
- Is the document formatted so it looks good?
- Will the document be easy to automate?
- Have you used pictures and tables to make key information understandable?
- Is the language as plain and simple as possible?
- How can I simplify that clause?
- Can I make that paragraph clearer?
- What parts of the document are always questioned?
- Would a table or flowchart explain this more clearly?
- What are the standard items we always negotiate?
- Are headings used clearly?
- Do I have the Reverse Sandwich Contract structure correct?

Outsource (Contract Document)

>> Key Question: Can someone else (or something else) do this task for me to create the final document faster?

Our document is singing! We have optimised it to be clear and understandable. When we turn to consider the outsourcing of the document, we are talking about the regular creation of a final document we can present to someone for signature.

Because we're thinking like lazy lawyers, you might have spotted a few opportunities along the way. Now we need to look at how the contract will interact with the contract process as we currently understand it.

We might not have a complete, detailed or exact picture of the entire contract process just yet. That's okay. We can build around the broad strokes we've developed from optimising the contract document and assessing the items which regularly change.

What would a diva do?

The key question we keep in mind as we review the contract document for potential outsourcing, 'What would Beyoncé do?'.

No just kidding, the key question is 'Can someone else (or something else) do this task for me to create the contract document faster?'

Other questions to consider...

- [ ] Can the customer or supplier enter that information themselves (e.g. phone and email addresses, site details, etc)?

- [ ] Could I give contract users a list of pre-approved clauses to negotiate on or a list of second positions they can adopt during negotiations?

- [ ] Can a paralegal review the request and ensure our template document is suitable?

- [ ] Would the marketing team, information designer or plain language expert be able to assist with making important clauses and timelines crystal clear?

- [ ] Can I link my electronic signature platform with a customer database (e.g. DocuSign talks to Salesforce)?

- [ ] Is there a way to sync my electronic signature platform up with an external database (e.g. abr.gov.au to check business numbers or Australia Post to check addresses)?

The SLAPP test

If it's hard to read, it's hard to do

Hyunjin Song and Norbert Schwarz

Is your contract document productive yet?

How do I know if my contract is productive after running it over with Triple O Productivity? You can test how well you've done at getting your contract document productive with a few easy tests. Just SLAPP your contract document into shape...

- ☐ Structure
- ☐ Likeable
- ☐ Automated
- ☐ Plain language
- ☐ Pictures and plans

The quick SLAPP

Five quick questions to test whether your contract is ready for the big wide world...

1. Is your contract structured like a Reverse Sandwich so it's useful and usable? (Structure)

2. Does your contract look good? (Likeable)

3. Is your contract ready for low-code automation? (Automated)

4. How easy is your contract to read and understand? (Plain language)

5. Do you use pictures, flowcharts, graphics, tables and other visuals to break up text? (Pictures and plans)

Structure

>>Key Question: Is your contract structured like a Reverse Sandwich so it's useful and usable?

Structure is key to creating a contract document that is usable and productive. If your structure is old fashioned or illogical, it reduces the readability and increases the time to negotiate, read and implement.

Words are important, structure is essential.

Hannah Morgan-Stone

Ask yourself:

- ☐ Have you structured the document in a way that makes sense?

- ☐ Is the contract document easy to follow?

- ☐ Does the structure work in a digital world?

- ☐ Can anyone open that contract and see what it is about?

- ☐ Will the structure of the document help people clearly see what's going on in the contract?

- ☐ Have I used numbering or alphabetical order to make sense of clustered information?

- ☐ Does the order of my contract terms follow the lifecycle of the contract relationship?

- ☐ Does the structure help me to automate the contract?

In Tactic 1, we learned the idea of making a Reverse Sandwich Contract™. This is the big structure secret for big productivity boosts. Reverse Sandwich Contracts™ mean you, your clients, and customers don't waste time looking for information. All the key parts of the agreement are easy to read and e-ready (i.e. ready for electronic processes and automation).

The basic structure of a Reverse Sandwich Contract™ is standard terms (that don't change) in the middle, important things we need to know and terms that do change on the top and bottom.

If you are interested in different structure concepts, check out the International Business Communication Standards Association (IBCS-A) approach to structuring documents.

Likeable

>>Key Question: Does your contract look good?

The way your document looks matters. If your document is easy on the eyes, people will prefer to read it. Whilst I am sure your contracts aren't written using Comic Sans font (goodness gracious, please tell me they aren't?!), things like font and formatting are so important.

Clutter and confusion are failures of design not attributes of information

Edward R Tufte

Having a likeable, good looking document ties in with making the contract easy to read (see *Plain Language* section below).

☐   Is the document formatted in a likeable way, does it look good?

☐   Do other people think it looks good?

☐   Have you used a sans serif font for an easy digital reading experience?

☐   How does your contract look?

☐   Have you asked the people who use the contract how they think it looks?

☐   What do customers think of your contracts?

Formatting Tips

There are many, many resources online about plain language and formatting (just search **plain language** resources and prepare yourself for sifting).

Some quick tips for formatting clear documents which I go by:

- Use a clean, sans-serif typeface (a.k.a. font) for easy on-screen reading (try Calibri, Verdana, Arial or Gill Sans)
- Use a font size between 10 – 12 pt
- Avoid italics and underlining (they are harder to read)
- Line spacing for contract text may depend on the document itself and the length. I like line spacing between 1.15 and 1.3 pt.
- Use 'Styles' and 'Levels' for easy scanning of headings and referencing the document overall.
- Leave some white space (I go for a 'Moderate' margin – see below)
- Group ideas sensibly, don't leave items on their lonesome (e.g. signature panels or tables split in half or headings without their clauses)
- Use style guides and learn basic formatting skills (for Microsoft Word or Google Docs)
- 'Moderate' is a good starting point for most documents.

The key is to check the presentation of ideas and concepts on each page.

Automation Ready

>>Key Question: Is your contract ready for low-code automation?

Here is where the contract document intertwines with the contract process. The way a contract process works can affect how a contract document is best structured. Try mapping out the process for contract creation to see how automation could affect the way you structure the document.

Depending on how the document works its way through different stages of contract approval or information gathering until fully completed, different structures may be required. Short and sharp items might be better at the front of the contract (Key Details) while others are better suited to the back (Schedules).

For example, important name and contact details are best placed at the front of the agreement, in tables for easy reference later on. If you need to add in the search records for a registered company search as part of the automated approval process, make sure your structure reflects this, with an annexure at the back of a schedule.

See *Productive contract process* section for more detail on process mapping to prepare for automation.

Plain Language

>>Key Question: How easy is your contract to read and understand?

Maybe you don't care; you only care about tying someone up in legal knots to protect your organisation to the maximum extent possible.

If that is your attitude (or the attitude of lawyers you know) then perhaps you need a plain language intervention. The costs of poor writing can really stack up — check your costs out using the ReWrite for Change calculators at rewriteforchange.com/calculators-2/.

Whilst there are some doubts thrown on the accuracy of different readability scales, standard tools that are freely available (such as the readability tools in Microsoft Word, the app Grammarly and others) give helpful guidance on how readable your contract is.

Aiming for a readability scale of grade level 9 ensures you writing will be almost universally understood. Push yourself to write simply and check your scoring.

'But I am simple in my communications!' I hear you say. Well, there is an easy way to check.

Go to your Sent email folder.

Find the last email you sent which had more than 3 sentences.

Head to www.webpagefx.com/tools/read-able/ and paste that text in.

Whilst the Java script used does not record or store any information entered – be on the safe side and de-identify any information.

What score do you get? A score level of 9 means your text can be pretty much universally read and understood. If you score over 9, your message is likely too complex to be rapidly understood and acted on.

It's quite hard to keep sentences short (especially when it feels like all the ideas should be clumped together).

You ~~have to~~ must cut ~~out all~~ unnecessary words.

Quick and easy plain language tips for writing simple contracts

- ☐ Use headings for easy reading and scanning
- ☐ Keep clauses short, sentences should no more than 20 words and around the 15 words per sentence mark
- ☐ Keep word syllable count low
- ☐ Use numbering and bullets wisely (like salt, not too much)

#Writelikeahuman

Shelley Davies

People work better together with clear & simple information. A study looked at using 'plain English' in written clinical guideline recommendations. The clear & simple guidelines 'led to stronger intentions to implement the guidelines, more positive attitudes towards them, and greater perceived behavioural control over using them.'

Simple communication is an easy way to foster a more positive attitude towards compliance and legal obligations.

Trust is a two-way street. If lawyers want to be trusted advisors, they need to earn that trust through clear & simple communications.

We sell products today which have more computing power than the rockets that put humans on the moon, yet they don't often come with manuals. Despite the complexity of these products, they are often easy to use at a basic level.

IKEA instructions manage to explain the building of various kind of furniture and accessories using only diagrams and pictures.

Imagine if your internal communications were read and understood the first time... How much extra time per day would you have? Learning new skills to write simply will give you you're your business!) massive productivity gains.

Writing simply for fellow team members is the right thing to do. Writing simply for customers is the right thing to do. Writing easy to read, simple legal contracts is the right thing to do.

The process may loop back

You're not going crazy if you find further things to obliterate once you run a plain language comb over your document. Optimising your contract document with plain language often overlaps with obliterating unnecessary clauses and words.

For example, in the course of optimising a contract clause with plain language, you might realise you don't actually need that clause after all. When language is simpler, we can see it clearly. When clauses are simplified, we notice we repeat ourselves or the clause is outdated or contradicts a later amendment or is just wrong.

If you find more unnecessary contract process steps or legal clauses to Obliterate, well done! That's the whole point.

What about legalease?

If you think you can't change a wordy word for a 'legal' reason, check out the next section for slightly more advanced plain language productivity, *Losing Legalese*.

Writing easy-to-read and simple legal contracts is the right thing to do.

Pictures and Plans

>>Key Question: Do you use pictures, flowcharts, graphics, tables and other visuals to break up text?

This isn't just for aesthetics; visual diagrams often clarify vague concepts. Key red flags to look out for are clauses with delivery requirements, dates or dollars. Pretty much anything with numbers is likely work better if placed into a table for easy reading at a glance.

...even highly educated people and [judges]... perform better with a visual contract...

Stefania Passera

The Picture Superiority Effect

The Picture Superiority Effect tells us that pictures are 6 times more likely to be remembered than words. This is an incredible superpower you can take advantage of for yourself, for your team, and for your clients.

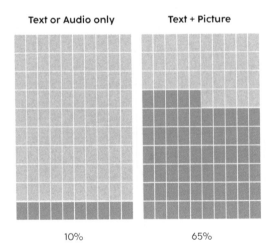

Memory retention after 3 days

Text or Audio only   Text + Picture

10%   65%

A visual notice clause

A bit of background first for those who aren't sure on what a notice clause is. Notice clauses are parts of a contract which tell the parties when a communication is considered delivered. Why do we need this kind of term?

Well, imagine I rent an office building and I have excellent, cheap rent. On top of cheap rent, I very cleverly negotiated myself an option to renew for another three years if I choose. My landlord isn't happy about this. Prices have gone up quite a bit. The price in my contract is capped at a 3% rent increase each year only. Huzzah. All I must do is notify the landlord I want to renew the lease before the deadline of 16 June 2017 and I'll have cheap as chips rent for three more years.

But... things got away from me so I left it to the last minute. I prepared the notice and sent it off via email on the morning of 16 June 2017, a Friday. The Landlord had taken the Friday and Monday off. On Tuesday, when the Landlord looked in her email she said 'Ah ha! You're too late! The notice needs two Business Days before it's delivered'.

'Oh no no my friend,' I said. 'Have a look at the bit about email delivery.' Luckily for me, I had created a gorgeous visual version of the wordy lease notice clause. Which of the below clauses do you prefer? Which one is faster and easier to read in a hurry?

BEFORE

Notices

(a) Any notice to be given to one party by another under this agreement must be in legible writing, in English and addressed to the intended recipient, and delivered to the recipient in person or by courier hand delivery, by prepaid ordinary post, by facsimile or by email, and must be signed by an authorised officer of the party giving or making it, or (on its behalf) by any solicitor, director, secretary or authorised agent of that party.

(b) A notice is regarded as being given by the sender and received by the recipient:

    (i) if by delivery in person, when delivered to the recipient;

    (ii) if by post, three Business Days from and including the date of postage;

    (iii) if by facsimile transmission, whether or not legibly received, when the machine from which the facsimile is sent generates a transmission report confirming that all pages of the notice have been sent to the recipient's facsimile number; or

    (iv) if by email, immediately unless sender receives an automated reply that the email was not delivered by reason of the address being invalid or otherwise.

(c) If a notice is received on a day which is not a Business Day or after 5:00pm on a Business Day, that notice is regarded as received 9:00am on the following Business Day.

AFTER

Notices

A party giving notice under this Agreement must do so in writing to the contact in the Agreement Details, or such other contact notified.

Method of notice	When is notice received?
MAIL (HAND DELIVERY) Left at recipient's address	Date of delivery.
MAIL (POST) Sent by post to recipient's address	3 business days after date of posting if sent by registered post, 4 business days if sent otherwise.
EMAIL Sent to recipient's email address	If sender's email system does not receive a delivery failure notification, the date the email is sent.

If a notice is received after 5pm or on a non-business day, then notice is received at **9am** on the **next business day**.

This is the kind of clause lawyers and others check often. It involves the normal, day-to-day operations of the contract itself. We need to make these day-to-day, operational clauses as clear as possible to make the contract truly useful and super speedy.

What did we do to the notice clause?

- Obliterated notice by fax machine – outdated technology and taking up valuable real estate.

- Obliterated duplication and confusing numbering.

- Optimised with plain language principles, switched legalese (deemed) to common sense (regarded as).

- Added clear headings and reduced confusing numbering systems.

- Inserted basic emojis to make the different types of communication delivery recognisable without reading; our brains understand images much faster than words.

- Used a table to separate out the information; our brains like to see what's the same and what's different.

- Made some things clearer, i.e. what happens if a notice is sent by normal mail and not registered post.

What clauses can you think of that would benefit from a bit of visualisation or tables?

Learn more about visual contracts by searching LinkedIn and Instagram for hashtag #visualcontract or visit the Checklist Legal website and search 'visual contracts'. Get inspiration from experts such as by Helena Haapio, Stefania Passera, and Robert de Rooy (known for developing Comic Contracts).

Explore the incredible work of Helena Haapio and Stefania Passera in the Contract Design Pattern Library, https://contract-design.worldcc.com/ .

The visual contract elicits more positive emotions (e.g. inspiration, determination, alertness) and fewer negative ones (e.g. hostility, frustration, shame) than the textual contract.

Stefania Passera

Pick low hanging fruit

On your first attempt, don't try to turn a mission critical document into a Reverse Sandwich. Gently ease your way in.

Just like a new year resolution to run a marathon, don't go for the full distance on day one. Stay away from massive wholesale agreements, personal guarantees, parent company guarantees, contracts that are often negotiated, documents with many changing schedules and other complicated contracts.

When your skills are refined, we can tackle these bigger challenges. Reverse Sandwich Contracting™ as a concept works on all contracts, large and small. But you must build up to it like any other skill.

Please get in touch if you come up against brick walls or aren't sure something will work; I love to problem solve these processes.

Ideas for contracts to start with (low hanging fruit)

Some great low hanging fruit documents to practice Reverse Sandwich Contracting on are:

- non-disclosure agreements (also known as NDAs or confidentiality agreements)

- internal approvals and sign-off sheets

- letters sent out in relation to larger agreements (such as performance warning letters, mutual termination letters, option exercise letters, etc)

- talent release forms

- marketing insertion orders

- low value settlement agreements

Basically, anything that is shorter than five pages, has only minor regular changes and only needs one or two signatures is a great place to start testing to see how much fiddly time and energy you can save.

LOSING LEGALESE

MINDSET:
Less legalese, more trust

Clients hate legalese

Clients dislike legalese.

Christopher R. Trudeau is a passionate plain language supporter, particularly for medical information. Trudeau has studied the public's language preferences and his work provides strong, empirical evidence in favour of plain language over legalese.

...the vast majority of clients and non-clients prefer plain language
...readers chose the plain-language version 80% of the time

Christopher R. Trudeau

Trudeau's study presented alternative versions of the same clause and asked people participating in the survey to select which they liked better. Two questions and the preference percentage results from his 2011 study are shown below:

LEGALESE		PLAIN LANGUAGE	
3%	I am herewith returning the stipulation to dismiss your case; the same being duly executed by me.	97%	I have signed and enclosed the stipulation to dismiss your case.
10%	If there is a continuation of this breach, my client will effect an immediate termination of this contract.	90%	If this breach continues, my client will immediately terminate this contract.

So, avoid your documents getting that 'musty legal smell', and drop the 'here-and-there' words. Clients will love you for it.

Why lawyers should hate legalese too

If the fact that clients hate legalese doesn't nudge you towards losing legalese, there are still more reasons to drop the legal lingo. Lawyers are human (mostly) and they work better with plain language just like non-lawyers. Trudeau has shown that clients and lawyers much prefer plain language over complicated legalese.

Even though they can understand legalese – although, like many dialects, there are differences even among lawyers on what particular words mean – even lawyers function better and prefer plain language over legalese.

> *...over 40% of clients had, at some point, stopped reading a document out of frustration.*
>
> *Christopher R. Trudeau*

Why would you write in a way that frustrates your intended audience? Why write documents which aren't readable?

For a lawyer, writing in plain language means their communications are easier to read. People much prefer things that are easy to understand. We don't just like easy to understand things, we also assess them as more positive in several different ways.

Things that are easy to read create 'mental shortcuts' – we are more likely to trust and like things that are easy to read and understand. This can flow through to being more trusted and being engaged to complete more work.

> *When your messages are easy to understand, they have a head start... you might even say it's an unfair advantage.*
>
> *Caitlin Whiteman*

But, surely I've got to have some bits of legalese!

Think there are some legal words that just must appear in contracts? Lawyers tend to exaggerate the extent to which the law requires specific legal wording for documents. Whether this is motivated by a desire to protect clients or protect their own business model, lawyers like to use specific 'legal words'. Keeping these words in documents reduces the documents' readability.

The law is no serious obstacle to writing clearly and plainly.

Joseph Kimble

Words to banish

There are many 'legal flavouring' words we can remove from our contracts. Words to banish include:

- ☐ deemed
- ☐ shall
- ☐ indemnify
- ☐ provided that

Deemed

If you see a lawyer use the word 'deemed', be fully prepared to fight back. Ask they change 'deemed' to 'considered as', 'is sufficient proof that' or 'regarded as'.

Why? Because it's confusing and even lawyers have to stop to consider what it means when reading it. Better to use the plain language version.

As far back as 1987, the Law Reform Commission of Victoria pronounced the word deemed as obsolete, and recommended drafters do not use it *even in the technical case of expressing a ... legal fiction*.

Ditch 'deemed'.

Shall

Depending on what you are trying to say, 'shall' might mean:

- has a duty to

- is required to

- should

- may

- will

- is entitled to

Why use a word with several different meanings? Why make your document unclear?

There is lots of commentary on how confusing 'shall' is but I think Joseph Kimble says it best: Give shall the boot; use must instead.

... use of jargon is a crutch ... a way of avoiding working harder ...

Bryan A. Garner

Indemnify

Around the world, 'Indemnification' clauses have been in the top three most negotiated clauses for the past decade.

The IACCM (International Association of Contract & Commercial Management) runs a regular survey of its global members. Two key questions in the survey ask which contract terms are the most heavily negotiated and which terms are the most important.

However, the very same term regularly fails to crack the top ten in terms of importance. Globally, we've wasted many, many hours negotiating terms which aren't considered important.

One reason 'indemnity' clauses are so heavily negotiated, is the word itself.

It is not certain. What does it mean? Often these clauses are a confusing mix of 'indemnified party', 'indemnification', and 'indemnity'. Jeffrey S. Ammon encourages lawyers to banish the word indemnity and rebuild indemnity clauses from scratch.

The simpler way to say indemnify? 'Pay for'.

Why write indemnify when you can say pay for?

Joseph Kimble

Provided that

It's been said that 'lazy drafters' make use of the term 'provided that' because they aren't exactly sure what they mean.

Try saying that to a lawyer and see what reaction you get!

Clauses with 'provided that' often contain exceptions or are extremely long and confusing – you forget the first part whilst trying to understand the exceptions. The reader is left to construct a mental Venn diagram of what the clause actually means. If you spot 'provided that', ask the writer to explain it or change it.

The best plain language version to use in place of 'provided that' is to 'say what you mean'.

More plain langugae

For further background on why the above words help no one and more law words you can cut, read Law Words: 30 essays on legal words & phrases by the Centre for Plain Language and comprehensive The A to Z of alternative words by the Plain English Campaign

You sound smarter if you use plain language

Legal flavouring is a term used to describe a word that 'either [adds] no meaning or [has] a perfectly acceptable plain English alternative'.

Just like too much salt in cooking, you need to watch the amount of 'legal flavouring' you add to contracts. Legal flavouring might make a contract taste good to the lawyer who wrote it, but to most other people, it's overpowering.

Legalese is made of 'empty words that don't have any persuasive character'

Barbara Lynn

In a study examining how the ease of reading affected peoples' perceptions of intelligence, Daniel M. Oppenheimer found that 'complexity negatively influenced raters' assessments of texts'. The more complex the text was, the less people liked it and the less intelligent they thought the writer was.

Oppenheimer concludes the reason simple texts are preferred over complex texts is fluency. Complex texts are difficult to read. Write clearly and simply if you can, and you'll be more likely to be thought of as intelligent.

Steer clear of legalese. Do the work to understand your reader and write for readability to gain trust.

Less legalese, more trust

PRODUCTIVE CONTRACT PROCESS

MINDSET:
Design for readability

Not Six Sigma certified... at all

A word of warning... I am not a management consultant or a process specialist. I can't tell you what Six Sigma is and I have never inspected a production line. There are some serious experts around who love granular detail of process mapping – that's not what this secret is about.

This secret is about simple process mapping tools and questions you can use right now (without a consultant or fancy software) to help rapidly outline process steps in complex contract relationships.

Getting in sync

By now, we are well on the way to thinking digitally about the contract work we do. We look beyond just our portion of the contract drafting or preparation. We understand a contract sits within a wider contract process. Sometimes we are aware of the processes before and after we see a contract. Sometimes we aren't.

When we apply Triple O Productivity to the contract process, we are engaging with our clients in a positive way, finding ways to make their work life easier and happier, as well as your own.

We are also on the look-out for potential minions so we can delegate like a diva.

Why is it so important that our contract process runs smoothly? Why not just worry about the contract document? Why do we need to get our contract process and contract document in sync?

What happens when your process and document are out of sync?

At the Athens Olympics in 2004, in the Women's 8s rowing final, a controversy erupted.

Despite a strong, synchronised start by the Australian team, who were rowing powerfully towards possible medal contention, at some point in the final 300 metres of the race, one athlete stopped rowing. This was unheard of at elite level rowing and had never been seen in Olympic history.

The remaining athletes tried encouragement, prodding, yelling. It didn't help. Sally Robbins had dropped her oar and stopped rowing. Robbins was dubbed 'Lay Down Sally' by various media outlets and criticised publicly by teammates, leading to a court case.

It's clear something went wrong for Robbins. Whether an athlete breakdown is physical or mental or even some combination of the two is beside the point.

The other athletes in the boat would later describe how they felt 'ripped off' and powerless. They felt 'frustrated and annoyed and pissed off'. They were in disbelief and they were embarrassed. Whilst we might never know what it's like to get to an Olympic Games, we can imagine how it would feel if we were in that boat after months of tough training and years of sacrifice.

The fact is, even though just one out of eight athletes was not in sync, it had a massive impact on the performance of the whole team. This is the same for contracting. You need to get your contract process and contract document to work smoothly and in synchronisation.

Does it really matter if the contract process doesn't match the contract document? Not entirely convinced? Alright, let's dive a bit deeper into how the contract process affects your productivity personally.

How contract processes affect productivity

Many businesses earn their revenue by reselling other companies' goods and services. From car dealerships to questionable 'nutrition' shakes, and all the way up to Amazon's robust affiliate marketing platform, external distribution channels have always been popular ways to scale business growth.

Affiliates and external sales channels are often tricky for lawyers or anyone working in compliance heavy areas.

Affiliates sell your products for you and you pay them a commission, but they aren't your direct employees. As an organisation, you have the benefit of less overheads but an increased risk caused by lack of control and less visibility.

People managing these external affiliate agents are often salespeople themselves, which brings with it another set of challenges. Good salespeople often promise the world because they are eager to please and show the capability of the organisation. In reality, things are often slower and less shiny than the picture a salesperson paints.

When it comes to getting a new external affiliate agent on board, timing is critical. When you think of it from the sales team's point of view, they are keen to get a new stream of sales coming in (and they have targets to meet). From the new affiliate's point of view, by committing to sell particular products, potentially on an exclusive basis, they (and their team) may be without steady income for a certain period - 'between jobs' so to speak - whilst the business is getting organised to bring them on board.

From my point of view, the standard agreements to get these new affiliates signed up were a hassle! There was no challenge, it was purely data entry and traffic direction. I knew it was important to get these agreements done quickly and I did want to help to get them done fast.

However, my inner three-year-old would say 'I don't wanna!' whenever a new request for one of these agent agreements would arrive in my inbox. Still, I generally got the documents out within one to two business days (or faster if the request was urgent). Fairly reasonable time frames.

Contracts and Legal staff are good at fixing problems. However, this ignores the point that many of those problems could have been avoided.

World Commerce and Contracting

After receiving complaints that 'legal is holding things up for weeks', I was surprised. I didn't think my part took very long, except perhaps when I needed to go back for further information — but that wasn't my fault, right?

I decided to investigate and mapped out the current process, asking questions and mostly asking why. Testing the reasons why each step in the process was needed.

- Why does the commission team need to approve the agreement if the fees are standard?

- Why does the new agent wait to complete training until the agreement is fully signed?

- Why does the legal team see the agreement before the Director approves the new partner?

- When does the new agent need access to systems?

- Why do we send the Agent an unlocked, editable copy of the agreement when we aren't really prepared to negotiate the terms?

- Why does the area manager need to approve the agreement?

- Can't we just notify them when the agreement is finalised?

- Why is the process linear?

- Does each step depend on the other or can finance and the legal team approve separately?

And more!

See below for further examples of questions for teasing out reasons behind contract process steps.

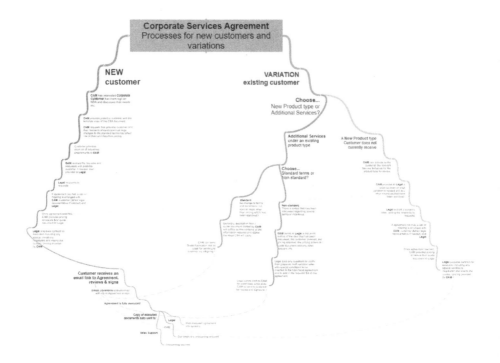

When I knew the process, I could see it wasn't 'legal' slowing the whole process down, it was a combination of each link in the chain taking a day or two extra to get the correct information they needed to do their piece of the on-boarding. There was also an issue of trust. Certain teams didn't trust the manager to use standard commission structures or terms. This meant these suspicious teams wanted to approve every document before and after it went to the new agent.

We solved these issues with the following workarounds.

Mapping the entire process visually

Everyone involved could see how their task contributed to the whole. So many times when I was discussing the process, someone would point at the mind map and say 'Huh, I guess I could just get a copy here at the end instead of the start if that's the approved version' or 'Gee I didn't realise the whole thing had that many steps' or 'I didn't know it came to legal before me; if it's legally approved I don't need to see it'.

Refining the application form

We reworked the application form so new agents gave us all the information we needed at each step to smoothly approve and create a new contract. They couldn't progress or finish the form unless they filled out each field.

We electrified it

With the process automated via DocuSign, we were now prompted if fields were left blank. We could also lock down the standard terms. This gave those suspicious teams comfort. They no longer wanted to approve before and after contract creation, they only wanted notification when new agent joined so they could provide systems access – all the information they needed was now automatically sent to them. Less work and less risk make compliance folk very happy.

Key negotiation areas

The biggest item which was often negotiated or discussed was exclusivity. This was a decision around whether the agent could only sell our products or whether they could promote competing products also. After discussing and training the team on the risks, pros and cons of exclusive agents, I put the power back into the hands of the sales manager with a tick box. It was easy to set up, the managers understood it, and new agents loved it because they felt they were getting something for their negotiating.

☐ *Check this box if clause 16 (Exclusivity) applies*

... all the users of a contract must row together with complete trust in each other, the contract document and the contract process.

As you can imagine, by getting all contract users to row together, we made the entire process much less stressful.

☐ **Approvals** – If you know who and what department needs to approve certain issues, you can more easily ask them questions about the contract directly as they arise.

☐ **Thresholds** – When you understand the process, you know the threshold issues of the stakeholders, which can help you provide clear advice about potential contract amendments.

☐ **Knowledge management and upskilling** – With an understanding of the pre-contract process, you can create useful tools for salespeople to help them manage customer expectations around legal negotiations. This gives your clients more skills and frees up your time from handling the same, low-value questions – it's a win-win!

☐ **Improve your contract document** – Understanding the contract process can show you more ways to streamline your document. There might be entire sections that aren't needed. Talking to the Contract Owners is an important way to understand the process and contract document better to improve both.

To operate at optimum productivity, all the users of a contract must row together with complete trust in each other, the contract document and the contract process.

How to get you contract processes in sync

To get in sync, we need to think about contracts differently. When contract users are rowing in sync...

- Each person trusts the contract document because it's easy to read, key information is easy to find, and the structure makes sense. Each person can trust the contract process because it is logical, makes sense and is transparent.

- Almost anyone can read the contract and explain its basic structure easily. Operations staff can understand key areas of the agreement and act on them.

- Positive customer experience moves smoothly from the presentation of a solution from a salesperson into the formal record of that agreement.

- Each person in the contract process has a sense of ownership over the contract document and process, not just the outcome or their particular area.

Lawyers and managers should understand each other's worlds as fully as possible.

Thomas Barton, Helena Haapio, and Tatiana Borisova

Don't put lipstick on a process pig

As we said before, don't put lipstick on a pig. This means don't bother trying to hide the true nature of something to make it gorgeous.

The first rule of any technology used in a business is that automation applied to an efficient operation will magnify the efficiency.

The second is that automation applied to an inefficient operation will magnify the inefficiency.

Bill Gates

A key aspect of Reverse Sandwich Contracts™ and the methods in this book is to really understand the document you are digitising. Not only that, you need to know the process that document goes through from go to whoa. That means talking to people, asking questions, listening. It might mean changing your processes to suit others, because it's faster overall.

If that's too much work for you, then stick with paper.

Reverse Sandwich Contracts™ aren't a magic wand. It isn't going to fix your terrible process for you. What it does do is highlight what the current processes are, allowing you to provide a better option.

Your contract document and contract process need to be solid

You need to have a 90% understanding of the whole contract process for Reverse Sandwich Contracting concept to really have a productive effect in your business.

If you don't know the process, set aside time, 20–30 minutes, to talk with people who use that contract regularly. This may involve salespeople who present the contract to the customer or the operations team who need to build what the customer has agreed to buy. Better still if you talk to both.

Examples of what you need to know:

- Who initiates the contract?
- What is normally negotiated?
- Who needs to sign it?
- Who needs a copy at the end?
- What changes?
- What stays the same?
- Which areas cause the most disputes?
- What areas of the contract are questioned?

There are robots you can train to do this analysis if you have the time and cash. We are going for low-code options to start with, to whip our contract process into shape.

Even the best coding, visualisation or legal writing is misplaced if it does not serve the needs of the audience, the clients or users.

Helena Haapio, Daniela Alina Plewe, and Robert deRooy

The groundwork you put in to understand a contract process can launch you into an 'Aha!' moment of clarity about the contract life-cycle as well as your client's motivations.

The fact you are asking for input into a contract from those that use the contract will have positive effects, increasing your reputation as a proactive and trusted advisor. Especially when you obliterate unnecessary steps.

Would clients or people in your organisation be shocked if you gave them an automated contract process and said 'If you use this contract and there are no changes to the standard, you don't need to come to legal. Just get it signed.'?

132

How would your business react? Can you hear yourself saying the above sentence or does it make you feel uneasy?

The groundwork you put in can launch you into an 'Aha!' moment of clarity about the contract life cycle and your client

Get it down and make it visual

Unclear contract processes delay contract turnaround. When you actually put pen to paper (digitally or literally) and map out a process for everyone to see, this issue become clear. Some will point to the process and say, 'That's not the approved process!'

Regardless of what the 'approved' or 'ideal' process is, getting down the actual process that really occurs is crucial for the below reasons.

You don't really know the game until you know the players

It's helpful if you can identify most of the key players in the lead up to getting a contract signed and actioned – these are the people you need to speak with about what they need from the contract (and they could also be future minions... remember Secret 2!)

Start a visual conversation

A visually mapped out process is a conversation starter. It says to your stakeholders that you care enough about them and their work and the contracts they use to create a useful visual tool.

Trust but verify

Your version of the process might be correct from your point of view, but someone else who uses that contract might be aware of another, side process that also happens. This is much easier to spot on a visual process map than a list of dot points. You might not learn about these silo processes without a visual map to talk to.

Prepare your requirements list

Because we're using the process map, you can also build out a requirements list. This can help if you want to move to a more high-tech solution down the track.

Evidence of how awesome you are

A mapped out visual process gives you a great starting point to show later when you've improved the process (everyone loves before and after photos!). This can be a great way to illustrate the value of making contracts more productive – they save not only legal time but processing time and resources across a company. Celebrate your successes visually!

This process is a mess – and you expect me to map it out?

Yes! It's easy to do with a few tools and the right questions. Process mapping is a serious business; it's beyond the scope of this book (and me!) to show you the best way to map your contract processes. The below tools will give you a great start on how to map a process and gather requirements to boost the productivity of your contract process.

Often a lawyer's process expertise is more important than legal expertise

Sarah McCoubrey

Okay so we know we need to map out processes, but how do we go about it?

Mind maps

What's a mind map? Great question! A mind map is an easy-to-use tool so you can 'brainstorm thoughts organically without worrying about order and structure. It allows you to visually structure your ideas to help with analysis and recall.'

At a basic level, a mind map can be pen and paper or a whiteboard and a marker. You pick a starting point – for example, a customer is interested in a product and a salesperson presents them with a contract – and map out each step in the process.

I think mind maps are excellent. Studies seem to show different levels of effectiveness for their use in students, but there's also a truckload of positive studies on mind mapping (from an admittedly biased but well-educated source, Tony Buzan, the 'inventor' of mind maps).

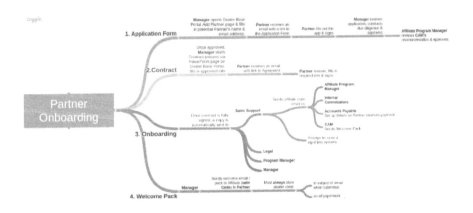

An example mind map for a basic contract process, from application form to approval, contract execution and welcome pack (Image credit: Verity White)

Pen and paper are fine or try sticky notes on a whiteboard. I love an online application called Coggle for quickly mapping out processes. Why are Coggle mind maps so great?

- they are easy to make (point and click, drag and drop, type, type, type)

- they look cool (pretty colours!)

- they are quick to make

- they are easy to change if the process changes (click, drag and drop)

- there's an app and they are online

- you can present on them if you need to without developing a dreaded, boring slide deck

- you can save them as an image or a PDF

- they feel brainstorm-y and collaborative when done in groups

You can upgrade from the free version to a premium Coggle account for around US$10 per month. This gives you greater storage of mind maps and other enhanced features.

How to create a contract process mind map

The below steps are based on Tony Buzan's '7 steps for Mind Mapping', tweaked for contract process mapping.

1. Start in the centre of the whiteboard or page.

If you are using pens, whiteboard markers or sticky notes, starting with the central idea in the middle gives you freedom to go anywhere with your lines and ideas. You might have process mapping on one side and random ideas you get for improvements along the way on the other side. Starting front and centre gives you space to think creatively. I work in Coggle, which has no real boundaries in any 2D direction. It also allows me to move branches around easily, add in emojis / icons and keeps my terrible handwriting a secret.

2. Name it and picture it.

Confidently write the contract you are mapping in the centre of the page, and if you can, draw a small picture (or use emojis) that are relevant to the agreement.

Images and headings help keep you focused on what you're mapping out.

3. Use different colours for different branches.

With different colours, you can highlight which processes are problematic (red) or working well (green). You can colour code branches by who is doing the task (different colour for each person). You can set aside a certain colour for questions that arise about this step in the process (I use pink!) so it's fast and easy to take notes that make sense later. Overall, colours make the whole map more interesting to take in and show to others.

4. Use curved branches, not straight lines.

Straight lines make your brain bored. Curve it up to help your brain ease along the process.

5. Limit each line to one distinct action that is undertaken in the process.

You don't need to go down to the level of click here, open this file, save file as kind of detail, but try to keep the 'tasks' as one line.

6. Work your way through the agreement steps, as you know them.

Build up the story of the contract process, as you currently see it. Go systematically from around the first interest in having a contract (e.g. a customer approaches a salesperson and they discuss a product purchase). It's good to go back a few steps before and after your current knowledge of contract creation to really help nut out links in the contract process chain.

After you have completed your initial draft, go through the mind map process again with other stakeholders, like an interview, and get feedback on how they see the process working.

Overview of sales process and documents

This document gives you an overview of the sales process and the documents that apply at each stage.

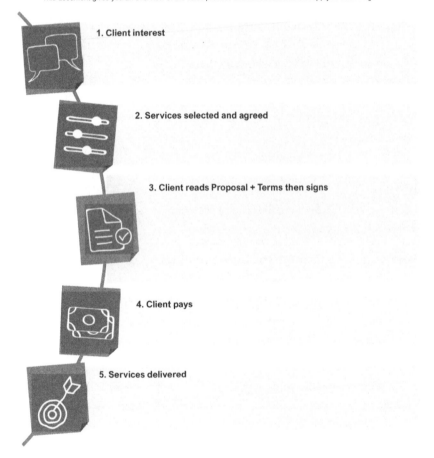

1. Client interest

2. Services selected and agreed

3. Client reads Proposal + Terms then signs

4. Client pays

5. Services delivered

Avoid the process pigs — low hanging fruit

Just like with our low hanging fruit documents, we want to start out with low hanging fruit process also if possible. We are just warming up in our Reverse Sandwich journey, so start small and work up.

Stick with documents that have linear workflows (i.e. I send to Justin, Justin fills in information signs and sends to Brittany, Brittany signs and we are done!). Use documents which do not need attachments.

Once you master the basics, you'll be process mapping like a pro and will easily spot areas you can speed up with Triple O Productivity.

If your process is simple and the contract is now structured correctly (Secret 1) and ready for electronic processes (Secret 4), there might not be much more for you to do in terms of Triple O Productivity for the contract process. When you work up to more complicated processes, you can come back and review Triple O Productivity for your contract process. Otherwise, feel free to skip ahead to the next section, Putting the secrets together.

Let's get stuck into the Triple O Productivity method for our contract process!

Obliterate (Contract Process)

>>Key Question: Do we need this step in the process? Can we do something else so this step isn't needed?

Just like when we applied the obliterate step to the contract document, we're now looking at the contract process to see what we need to get rid of.

Other questions to consider:

- Which area (or person!) holds up the process?
- Can we cut that person out of the process?
- Which tasks take the longest?
- Do we need that task fully completed or can it be shortened?
- What would happen if we didn't do that task?
- Can we get rid of this step or combine it with another to streamline the process overall?
- Does finance need to sign off if the contract is based on locked-down, pre-approved pricing?
- Is there consistently missing information, duplication, multiple locations for the same data, etc.?
- At what point in the process do you wait for someone to make a decision?
- At what point is information provided or put somewhere (for example, an inbox)?
- Where are the approvals and are they all needed?

Optimise (Contract Process)

>> Key Question: Now we are left with only the necessary process steps, is there a way to make every step in the contract process smooth, simple and speedy?

Is there a way to improve on the steps we absolutely need to have? If you must get approval by finance, what's the best way to go about it (e.g. send the request to a general inbox, a single person or provide other notice? Do we need their approval always or only over a certain threshold?).

We are looking to make every necessary step in the contract process as smooth, simple and speedy as possible for each person in the chain.

Other questions to consider:

- Which tasks add the most value to the contract process?
- Who owns those high-value tasks?
- Do we need that many rounds of negotiation?
- Could we set a cap on the number of negotiation rounds?
- Can you challenge the idea that one person cannot perform more than one step in sequence? Perhaps several things can be actioned at once?
- To reduce the number of handoffs, what do you need? (training, pre-approved levels, help from IT)
- Could the finance team provide pre-approval for contracts under a certain amount?
- Perhaps particular approvals aren't needed if the contract is a renewal or a variation?
- Who needs a fully signed copy?
- Can we add people who need a signed copy at the end of the workflow to automatically receive one?
- What steps in the process take the longest and can we speed them up?

Outsource (Contract Process)

Key Question: What parts of the contract process are best completed by...

- a Robot Minion?

- a Contract Owner Minion?

- a Customer Minion?

- a Minion Minion?

- Me?

We've structured our contract like a Reverse Sandwich and we are thinking like a lazy lawyer, constantly on the lookout for minions (human or robot) to speed up the contract process for all.

Delegating to the right technology or people (minions!) helps speed up the necessary steps in a contract process. Automating the contract process is one of the beauties of going digital.

Other questions to consider:

- Can I provide options for different situations (so lawyer's help isn't needed)?

- Do I need to be entering this data or can someone else enter it then I check over it?

- Can a paralegal approve this or does it have to be a lawyer?

- If the standard template is used, does this need to come to legal?

- Do I have to send a reminder email or can the application send that for me?

- Can an application automatically email and notify each person who needs notification?

Get curious about the contract process before and after you deal with the contract

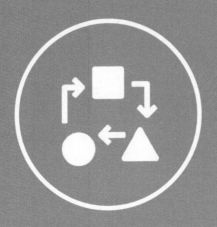

MAJOR MAPPING

MINDSET:
Complex not complicated

It is not enough to know how to write well; one should also learn to engage others in the process, elicit information, and communicate the core message effectively to the different readers.

Thomas Barton, Helena Haapio, and Tatiana Borisova

Simplifying complexity

I'm not living in a dream world. Having worked at large publicly listed companies with high regulatory scrutiny, I understand that some processes are more complex than others.

Complex processes can come about in lots of ways. From complex business rules to complex products and services, to high risk environments or shifting landscape of new laws.

Complexity can build up slowly overtime until one day it seems like a brick wall of confusion but those who built the wall say *'We've always done it that way.'*

When there are more cooks in the kitchen, there are more balls in the air and a higher chance of bottlenecks (+ increased rate of clichés!).

So where to start?

Once you have the general overview of the process end-to-end (i.e. in a mind map or simply in dot points), it helps to break down the process more formally so each player can see their exact role. This is more important for the chunkier processes with many moving parts. You might not need this if the mind map is clear, there are not many people involved, or the steps are relatively simple and linear.

Swim Lane diagrams are useful when there are several independent actions needed by different players at separate times. The basic idea of a Swim Lane diagram is that the process moves forward and we can see who is responsible for which part of the process depending on whether or not the task sits in their lane.

Franchise agreements are often very long by themselves but are also weighed down by strong laws which cover the kinds of information which potential franchisees must be given. There are also timing factors where a potential franchisee must receive certain information and then have 14 days to review that information.

I first got into Swim Lane diagrams when I wanted to give the key Franchisee contract process players a checklist for all the items they needed to complete to successfully set up a new franchisee. It took a fair bit of mapping and many discussions but we got there in the end. The result was a colourful diagram where each person could look for their lane and colour to confirm what they needed to do.

Swim lanes

There are some fancy applications you can use to map out swim lane processes which look fantastic in the demo but are much harder to build from scratch. So, I made my own basic version in Excel. You can download a copy of the very basic template from createcontractsclientslove.com

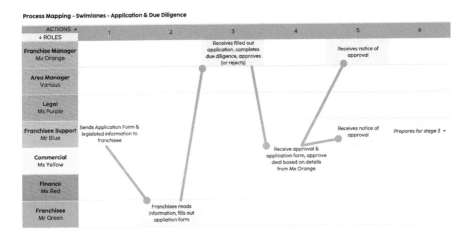

Head to the Create and Automate Better Contracts resource page to get a copy of this spreadsheet template.

As you can see, it's pretty simple! Each person who needs to approve or see a copy of the contract is down the left side. Each part of the contracting process is slotted into the relevant lane, depending on who completes the task.

Some of the process players want to receive notifications at every stage. This might be needed at the start, so include these information alerts to begin with. Once people start to trust the process and understand the steps it has gone through, you can Obliterate these further steps in the contract process.

So now we know the tools we can use and the basic process of mapping processes, what are we looking for along the way? What are the questions we need to ask ourselves and our stakeholders to correct a problematic process?

Each of these areas are closely related again. When you optimise one area of a process, it might mean that process can now be outsourced. Work your way through your process map, focussing on the tasks that slow the process down. Challenge yourself and the task owners to explain the reason why that task takes so long.

Try the 'ask why five times' method for root cause analysis if you aren't getting anywhere, and use the *Checklist for Common Process Problems* on the next page.

Common contract process problems checklist

Still having problems with contract processes? Remember to work through the Triple O method for each step in the contract process and have a visual map of the end-to-end process.

Process is too slow

If people keep complaining the contract process is too slow:

☐ Who owns those contract process steps that are slowing everyone down? Check in with them and ask how you can make life easier or speed things up for them.

☐ Reduce the number of people in the process.

☐ Gather clear and accurate information as early as possible (see below).

☐ Try to link in with an existing customer database to reduce data entry (which people find boring and often put off).

Missing or inaccurate information

If problems involve missing or inaccurate information:

☐ Require all information from clients or customer before the contract process kicks off (i.e. in an application form or other collection method).

☐ Add hard stops that don't allow people to proceed without entering required information.

☐ Use drop down menus or check boxes instead of free text fields to eliminate errors and speed up data entry.

☐ Create and report on measurements for information accuracy.

What are we putting together?

First, we met our productivity powerhouse, the Reverse Sandwich Contract™. We learnt the basic concept and structure of a Reverse Sandwich Contract™ and why it makes for a tasty contracting experience.

Then, our second tactic got us to start **thinking digitally** about how we work with contracts and contract users.

We understand from secret four we apply Triple O Productivity to everything we touch – the contract document and contract process – to streamline our contract into a productivity producing beast.

We understand we can't put lipstick on a pig of a process and expect miracles. We do the work to understand the contract process before we try to palm off our process problems to software or our contract users.

We Obliterated everything we don't need from our contract process and contract document. We Optimised the document to be as easy to read as possible (and then SLAPPed it to make sure). We know we can **SLAPP** our contract document into shape if we ever want to do a quick productivity check-up on the contract document to make sure it's easy to read and use for all.

We **Optimised** the process to be as smooth as possible with the least number of steps. We channelled our inner **diva** to **Outsource** parts of the contract document creation and aspects of the contract process to ready and (mostly) willing human and robot **minions**.

Now, it is time to put all the secrets together and make our very own Reverse Sandwich Contract™.

PUTTING ALL THE SECRETS TOGETHER

MINDSET:
Making contract design magic happen

Making a Reverse Sandwich Contract™ — the high-level process

STEP 1

THE STANDARD CONTRACT

Contract document and process are complex, hard to use, slow, confusing, and important terms are hidden.

STEP 2

OBLITERATE

Remove parts of the contract you don't need. Get rid of legalese. Remove unnecessary steps in the process.

STEP 3

OPTIMISE - QUICK WINS

Improve the structure and format of the contract document. Reduce legalese and refine the structure of your contract to suit your process and users.

STEP 4

OPTIMISE - DEEP DIVE

Dive into the details. Look at past experience and talk with people who use the contract. Continue to improve the document and process.

Remember to SLAPP your contract... Structure, Likebility, Automation, Plain language, and Pictures.

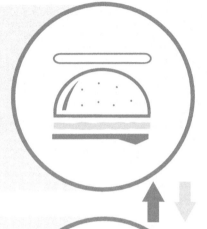

STEP 5

OUTSOURCE

Find minions (people or robot) to do tasks needed in creating the contract. Develop your plan for automation process in your chosen platform.

STEP 6

REFINE

Refine the contract document and contract process over time... at least once a year to keep on top of productivity and changes in business practices!
This may mean revisiting each of the steps to further refine the contract document and contract process.

OUTRO-DUCTION

MINDSET:
Go out and do it

Now it's your turn to create and automate

I hope I have inspired you to try and get more clarity in your business with contract design and digital tools!

- [ ] Try Reverse Sandwich Contracting™

- [ ] Think about contracts (and life!) digitally

- [ ] Map and fix those process pigs for speedy business

- [ ] Make your contracts easy to like for happy clients and customers

- [ ] Test out different automation software and see what you like (most of them have free trials)

- [ ] Let's connect on the socials! Search @checklistlegal and join the contract design conversation with the following hashtags #contractdesign #legaldesign #visualcontracts #reversesandwichcontracts

Your contract design and automation to do list

1. Make a reverse sandwich contract

Useful and usable | Structure your contract for the future to get productivity wins on the board, fast.

2. Remember your contract is not a bit of paper

Think digitally | Start thinking digitally to see your contract (and life!) for what it really is and what it can be.

3. Be a lazy lawyer

Delegate like a diva | Learn to automate and outsource. Lookout for minions (human and robot) who can effectively do a contractual task, leaving you to increase your skills in higher value areas.

4. Use Triple o productivity

Write for readability | Obliterate, Optimise and Outsource your contract document for massive productivity gains. SLAPP your contract into shape. Use the SLAPP system's five key document angles to confirm your contract document is at its productive peak – Structure, Likeability, Automation, Plain language, Pictures.

Be curious | Obliterate, Optimise and Outsource your contract process for an ongoing efficiency pay off. Don't put lipstick on a process pig! Fix your contract processes.

RESOURCES: THE BITS AT THE BACK

MINDSET:
Tools of the trade

Templates for reverse sandwich making

Electronically optimised key details table

The Key Details table is key to making your agreement flexible and scalable. Get these templates in a downloadable and editable format online.

The Key Details table is the front part of your Reverse Sandwich Contract. This is the tasty 'good stuff' that you want to know about a contract. The Key Details table is one of two places where you put all the key information about the agreement (the other is at the back in a Schedule – best used for larger amounts of information such as commission tables)

This form is easily filled out within your chosen electronic signature platform (or even with restricted Word editing). When the key details of an agreement can be filled out in the one spot, your contract becomes scalable, repeatable, accessible, easy to navigate and practically future-proof!

KEY DETAILS TABLE	
Start Date	[*The date the last party signs this agreement*]
Initial Term	[*5 years from the Start Date*]
Commission	[*See Schedule 2 (Commissions) for details* or insert $xxx per unit sold]
Confidential Information	[insert your preferred definition of Confidential Information]
Approved Purpose	[*e.g. To enable a party to disclose confidential information to the other party in the course of their employment relationship.*]
Payment Terms	[Insert payment terms]
Special Conditions	[Insert any negotiated conditions that are different than your standard terms or, for lengthy conditions, refer to a schedule and insert the details there, *See Schedule 1 (Special Conditions)*]

Below are two sample Key Details tables to give you some idea of what normally goes in. Basically, you can put in anything that changes regularly that can be described succinctly.

The definitions can refer back to the Key Details table to confirm the definition of the terms that apply. e.g. Start Date means the date outlined in the Key Details table at the front of this Agreement.

If you aren't using electronic contract templates or automated workflows yet, structuring your contracts with a Key Details sections as tables this way makes it much faster to prepare the contract, faster to find information later and faster for everyone to read.

Don't limit your use of Key Details tables to just long agreements. I love using Key Details as a concept within letters, notices and variations, even emails. Having the key information in a table and standard information below changes in one spot that is easy to find makes these small documents a breeze too!

KEY DETAILS TABLE

Start Date	15 June 2021
Initial Term	24 months
Commission	See Schedule 2 (Commissions)
Permitted Services	All Services advertised on the Supplier's website
Payment Terms	14 days from the date the invoice is sent via email.
Special Conditions	The following special conditions apply to this agreement: (a) Clause 6 (Exclusivity) does not apply to this agreement. (b) In Clause 24 (Definitions) of this Agreement, the definition of Approved Parties deleted and replaced with the following definition: *Approved Parties means the employees, representatives, subcontractors and related bodies corporate of the Supplier.*

KEY DETAILS

Start Date	The date the last party signs this agreement.
Term	12 months from the Start Date.
Confidential Information	Any information provided or accessed during the Term of this agreement which is not currently available to the public.
Approved Purpose	Discussions and negotiations around an agreement for the potential supply of products and services.

Electronically optimised schedules

Working in harmony with the Key Details table are the Definitions and Schedule sections of your agreement. The schedules at the back of your Reverse Sandwich Contract can work for almost whatever you want!

It could be a place for you to keep any terms that are negotiated, leaving you to clearly see what's changed from the standard.

SCHEDULE 1 – SPECIAL CONDITIONS

Special Conditions

The following Special Conditions form part of this Agreement:

(a) Clause 6 (Exclusivity) does not apply.

(b) X

(c) Y

(d) Z

SCHEDULE 2 – AUTHORISED PRODUCTS

The Agent is authorised to promote the Products in the below table and will receive the commission amount detailed in the below table for each Eligible Sale:

	Product	Commission for each Eligible Sale
1	Comb	$211
2	Brush	$287
3	Hat	$223
4	Feather	$250

Experiment with what works for you. A word of warning... as your schedules start getting bigger and bigger, they can get confusing and can slow you down.

Remember to keep your sandwich tight, move standard terms to the middle wherever possible.

Sample signature page

The signature page is key! Obviously, a contract needs to be signed; that's what we are looking for to confirm agreement to the terms.

If you do nothing else to your contracts, future-proof your execution pages. Even if everything else is manual, an easy way to apply signatures, dates & names will mean electronic signing is easier & clear. Get these templates in a downloadable and editable format online.

Note: Different applications have different ways of using signature panels. The below works excellently in DocuSign and several other applications. Some electronic contracting platforms (such as Concord) build the signature panel for you - handy! – so try a few out, see what works best for you.

They might not look like much but these signature panels are real time savers!

Executed on behalf of **Customer** by an authorised representative:

Signature

Name

Role

Date

Executed on behalf of **Supplier** by an authorised representative:

Signature

Name

Role

Date

Key features of these execution panels / signature sections...

☐   They don't take up much room in the document;

☐   They don't need updating each time for different contracts - just define the parties signing earlier in the agreement (preferably in a Parties table);

☐   The format works in electronic signature platforms as a template, just drop in form fields;

☐   The format works outside of electronic templating too. Paralegals or contract managers can fill out details faster with this format than traditional signature panels.

Sample parties sections

Often agreements will bury the contracting parties in recitals, in an opening paragraph, in the definitions section, or the contract dedicates a whole page to this information. Sometimes the contact person is buried in the middle of the contract in the notices section. All of that means more manual work which isn't scalable.

By placing the people & companies signing the contract into tables (see below), you can build out a template in your chosen electronic signature platform and to speed up the contracting process with automation and delegation to minions..

If you aren't using electronic contracts just yet, structuring your Parties sections as tables this way makes it faster to prepare the contract, faster to find information later and faster for everyone to read. If you are concerned about defining the parties, refer back to these tables in your definitions. e.g. Customer means the company outlined in the Customer table at the front of this Agreement.

Customer

Company	
Company Number	
Address	
Contact for Notices	Name
	Role
	Email
	Phone

Supplier

Company	
Company Number	
Address	
Contact for Notices	Name
	Role
	Email
	Phone

Quick wins checklist

Quick wins are good wins! Change up or delete these things from your contracts now for easy wins.

If you love checklists, visit www.createcontractsclientslove.com for more ticking goodness.

Front pages

Just get stuck into it! A heading is fine but don't waste people's time with a page turn.

Index

Do you need an index if your document is relatively short and searchable with clear headings? Would a visual overview of the contract structure be easier to understand?

Old fashioned fonts

No Times New Roman. Use Arial, Calibri, Gadugi, Gill Sans... basically any Sans Serif font works well on screens for easy electronic reading.

Two or more signatories | Witnesses

Signing a document with two or more people is generally a waste of time. In Australia, this is often referred to as means signing under section 127 Corporations Act (check your jurisdiction). One signature is faster than two! Change to just Authorised Representative (i.e. section 126 Corporations Act).

Is a witness really needed for your document? Especially if the contract is timestamped / geo-stamped / has 2-factor authentication? Fewer signatures means a faster, more productive contract.

Changeable terms

If terms throughout your agreement change (e.g. definitions, initial term clauses, company names, etc) or are regularly negotiated (e.g. payment terms, performance targets, exclusivity), get them up the front into your Key Details table.

Numbers

Pricing and commissions and targets... If it is a lot of numbers, it's likely to change. Develop standard tiers if possible and stick them into schedules at the back.

Negotiated special terms

Stop editing within an agreement. No one can pick up that document and see how it was negotiated. Put special conditions and changes to the standard document up the front so they are easy to see (good for a few special conditions); or consider 'standard' negotiated special conditions (better if lots of made often)

Always negotiated

Consider softening the standard position on difficult clauses which are often negotiated

Legalese and wordiness

Use plain language skills and tools to fix up the middle of a reverse contract sandwich. Try word swap lists: plainlanguage.gov/howto/wordsuggestions/simplewords.cfm

Legal referral service

For those living in Australia, many of the law associations offer free referral services. See below links for more information:

- ☐ Justice Connect (Australia Wide) | justiceconnect.org.au/get-help/referral-service

- ☐ Pro Bono Centre | probonocentre.org.au/legal-help/pro-bono-referral-schemes-and-organisations/

- ☐ Victoria | liv.asn.au/find-a-lawyer

- ☐ New South Wales | lawsociety.com.au/community/findingalawyer/solicitorreferralservice/

- ☐ South Australia | lawsocietysa.asn.au/referral

- ☐ Northern Territory | lawsocietynt.asn.au/for-the-profession/services-for-practitioners-4/legal-referral-service-2.html

About the author

Verity White is a commercial lawyer turned legal innovation expert with a passion for redesigning legal documents, contracts, and processes to be easy to read, easy to use, and jargon-free.

After 10+ years in corporate law land, Verity saw a problem. Too many business owners and lawyers were held back by confusing contracts and clunky legal processes. So, she started Checklist Legal to put her love for problem-solving and fixing things to good use. And to help change the world of contracting for the better!

Now, Verity is a multi-award-winning lawyer, legal innovator, and speaker sharing her love for clear, clever contracts with businesses and lawyers around the world. As an Honorary Senior Fellow at the University of Melbourne, Verity teaches Contract Design for Automation and is helping shape a new generation of lawyers (and contracts!).

When she's not trying to revolutionise the legal industry, you'll find her going all-out for a themed costume party (yes, even on zoom), walking a very cute Cavalier, or mixing up her go-to cocktail, a margarita.

Listen to Verity talking contract design on the Checklist Legal Podcast

Verity hosts the Checklist Legal podcasts and talks through contract simplification and contract design topics in a practical, straightforward, and engaging way.

The Checklist Legal Podcast is available via Spotify, iTunes, and your other fave podcast players.

www.checklistlegal.com/podcast

Want some help with re-designing your contracts for automation?

Perhaps you know your contracts are causing problems and you want them to be better, but you don't know where to start.

Verity and Checklist Legal can help no matter what level of contract design or legal tech you are working with.

✓ **Presentations and workshops**

✓ **Plain language review**

✓ **Contract mini-makeover**

✓ **Visual legals**

✓ **Process mapping**

✓ **Facilitation and designing project success**

✓ **Measuring success and benchmarking**

✓ **Automating preparation and execution**

✓ **Creating ongoing success with user & client guides.**

Tailored contract design projects often involve a combination of the above services, packaged up together with DIY or 'done for you' options.

Reach out to Verity via checklistlegal.com or let us know a little more about you by scanning the below QR code and let's talk contracts!

This QR code links to the Checklist Legal client enquiry form

References and further reading

INTRODUCTION

World Commerce and Contracting, 'Most Negotiated Terms Report 2020', worldcc. com/Portals/IACCM/Resources/9934_0_Most%20Negotiated%20Terms%202020.pdf.

Stanford Law School, 'CodeX Techindex' (Techindex) techindex.law.stanford.edu/ companies?category=2 accessed 9 February 2020.

See for example, Eric Chin, 'Build, Borrow or Buy: Three LegalTech Strategies for Law Firms' (Alpha Creates, 19 January 2019) alphacreates.com/build-borrow-or-buy-three-legaltech-strategies-for-law-firms/ accessed 9 February 2020; Erick Costa Damasceno, Business Models in Legal Tech Companies (Maria Raquel Guimarães ed, University of Porto 2019).

SECTION 1: THE BITS AT THE FRONT

PBS, Public Broadcasting Service, Transcript of interview with Elizabeth Warren (2 January 2009) Retrieved via pbs.org/now/shows/501/credit-traps.html, accessed 26 May 2017.

U Jagose, 'Clarity in legal language in English: Is it possible?' Presentation at Clarity 2016, Clarity International Conference, Wellington New Zealand, 2 – 5 November 2016. Retrieved via youtube.com/watch?v=AkzZQ8sUrDs, accessed 27 May 2015.

JS Poor, 'Re-Engineering the Business of Law' (7 May 2012) NY Times DealBook. .

Arkadi Kuhlmann is the former CEO of ING Direct in Canada and USA – founded six banking startups.

For a general overview on the Pareto Principle see betterexplained.com/articles/ understanding-the-pareto-principle-the-8020-rule/ and en.wikipedia.org/wiki/ Pareto_principle . For application of the principle in business, there are many sources, however I especially like Perry Marshall's longevity in this area and enthusiasm perrymarshall.com/80-20/ and Mark Manson's new spin on the old clichés markmanson.net/80-20-your-life.

SECTION 2: THE REVERSE SANDWICH CONTRACT

H Haapio, 'Designing Readable Contracts: Goodbye to Legal Writing—Welcome to Information Design and Visualization," (2013), IRIS 2013 at p. 447.

PJ Grosley, 'Tour to London' (1772).

NAM Rodger, 'The Insatiable Earl - A Life of John Montagu, 4th Earl of Sandwich' (1994).

S Covey, 'First Things First', (1994). For further information, visit the book website: stephencovey.com/firstthingsfirst/

E F Schumacher, 'Small Is Beautiful: A Study of Economics As If People Mattered', (1973).

Fitzroy Legal Service, The Law Handbook, 'What is a contract' (2020), lawhandbook. org.au/2020_07_01_00_how_contract_law_works/, accessed 18 Apr 2021

R Susskind and D Susskind, 'The future of the professions: How Technology Will Transform the Work of Human Experts' (2016).

Econsultancy, 'Internet Statistics Compendium' (September 2013)

A Singhal and M Cutts, 'Using site speed in web search ranking' (9 April 2010) and P Robles, 'It's official: Google incorporates website speed into your ranking' (12 April 2010) econsultancy.com

See also N Patel, 'How Loading Time Affects Your Bottom Line' blog.kissmetrics.com/ loading-time/ and R Whittington, 'Is A Slow Website Costing You Sales?'.

C Whiteman, 'Why easy-to-read is easy to like — what science tells us about the remarkable benefits of simplicity', (21 March 2016).

SECTION 3: A CONTRACT IS NOT A BIT OF PAPER

K Dorner and D Edelman, 'What digital really means' (27 February 2016).

H Haapio, and DA Plewe, and R deRooy, 'Contract Continuum: From Text to Images, Comics, and Code' (February 23, 2017).

For an in-depth look (and I mean in-depth!) at the differences between the A4 paper size and the Letter paper size, read betweenborders.com/wordsmithing/a4-vs-us-letter/ by Brian Forte.

For an excellent overview on building digital skills in an organisation, complete with great visuals on different approaches, see Delloite's 'Building your digital DNA: Lessons from digital leaders'.

E Brynjolfsson and A McAfee, 'The Second Machine Age: Work, Progress, and Prosperity in a Time of Brilliant Technologies' (January 2016)

SECTION 4: BE A LAZY LAWYER

Omaha World Herald, 'To Solve Hard Problem, Give It to 'Lazy Man'' (1 February 1947) CTPS News Service, Omaha, Nebraska. See also quoteinvestigator.com/2014/02/26/ lazy-job/#note-8269-3 for differing origins of this 'get a lazy person to do a hard job' quote.

M Tallarico, 'The creative minds and confidants that make up Beyoncé's entourage' (27 April 2016) Hello Magazine ca.hellomagazine.com/celebrities/02016042725914/inside-beyonce-s-entourage%20/ accessed 21 May 2017.

Henchmen from 'Austin Powers: International Man of Mystery' (1997). See also austinpowers.wikia.com/wiki/Steamroller_Henchman. Minions from 'Despicable Me' (2010).

See Merriam-Webster Dictionary, merriam-webster.com/dictionary/minion and N Whitman, 'The meaning of minion', Quick and Dirty Tips, published on Grammar Girl, 13 March 2015 quickanddirtytips.com/education/grammar/the-meaning-of-minion.

N Malone 'Can Women Have It All? Beyoncé Says Yes', New Republic (27 January 2013).

DocuSign, https://support.docusign.com/guides/cdse-user-guide-templates-creating-a-template

K Kelly, 'Robots will take our jobs', Gear (24 December 2012) wired.com/2012/12/ff-robots-will-take-our-jobs/, accessed 27 May 2017.

The Princess Bride (1987). If you are a Princess Bride fan, definitely check out princessbrideforever.com/, accessed 27 May 2017.

KL Milkman, JA Minson, and KGM Volpp, 'Holding the Hunger Games Hostage at the Gym: An Evaluation of Temptation Bundling'. (6 November 2013). For an interesting overview of 'temptation bundling', listen to the Freakonomics podcast episode 'When willpower isn't enough' freakonomics.com/podcast/when-willpower-isnt-enough-a-new-freakonomics-radio-podcast/

SECTION 5: TRIPLE O PRODUCTIVITY

Alan Siegel, CEO of Siegelvision, is a strong plain language advocate. Check out his TED talks on legal jargon and document design ted.com/speakers/alan_siegel, accessed 7 June 2017.

D Allen, 'Getting Things Done: The Art of Stree-Free Productivity' (2001). See also the book website gettingthingsdone.com/

F Heylighen and CF Vidal, 'Getting Things Done: The Science behind Stress-Free Productivity' (December 2008). Long Range Planning: International Journal of Strategic Management. 41 (6): 585—605.

Some of my favourites are Nozbe, Evernote evernote.com/, Coggle, Tasks in Microsoft Outlook, and Microsoft OneNote. See lifehacker.com.au/?s=GTD for more Getting Things Done hacks and systems.

M Sliwinski, 'Priority tasks instead of Next Actions...' (21 July 2014).

A Meisel, 'Less Doing, More Living: Make Everything in Life Easier' (3 April 2014). See also Ari Meisel's virtual assistant business Get Leverage getleverage.com/

IACCM (International Association of Contract & Commercial Management), 'Top Negotiated Terms 2015: No News Is Bad News' (21 January 2016) iaccm.com/resources/, accessed 10 June 2017.

For help with tracked changes in Microsoft Word see support.office.com and for Google Docs see docs.google.com/

SECTION 6: PRODUCTIVE CONTRACT DOCUMENT

C Whiteman, 'Why easy-to-read is easy to like — what science tells us about the remarkable benefits of simplicity', (21 March 2016).

C Schofield, 'Taming the sharks - driving business and illuminating the law' (November 2016) Presentation at Clarity2016, Wellington, New Zealand. See also clarity2016.org/taming-the-sharks.

H Song and N Schwarz, 'If it's hard to read, it's hard to do: Processing fluency affects effort prediction and motivation' (2008) Psychological Science 19(10): 986–988.

H Morgan-Stone, 'Plain to all: Using logic to distill complex thinking into clear documents' (November 2016) Presentation at Clarity2016, Wellington New Zealand.

ER Tufte, 'Envisioning Information' (1990). See also the book website for visuals: edwardtufte.com/tufte/books, accessed 10 June 2017.

See generally Geoffrey Marnell (excellent not only for the title pun but also the content) 'Measuring Readability, Part 1: The spirit is will but the Flesch is weak', and 'Advantages and disadvantages of readability formulas'.

Shelley Davies is an avid promoter of plain language and writing like a human. Check her work out at shellydavies.co.nz/

NA Merola, 'We like people who are easy to read: The influence of processing fluency in impression formation; (2014) PhD thesis, University of Texas.

S Michie and K Lester, 'Words matter: increasing the implementation of clinical guidelines', (2005) Quality & Safety in Health Care 14:367–370.

S Passera, 'Contract visualization - boost your brand and bridge the language barrier' (10 December 2014).

DL Nelson, US Reed, and JR Walling, 'Pictorial superiority effect' (1976) Journal of Experimental Psychology: Human Learning and Memory, 2, 523-528. For a visual overview of the Picture Superiority Effect, see DigitalSplashMedia's fun animation on YouTube youtube.com/watch?v=cLLDUyy8utY.

A great place to start on the journey of visual contracting is with the following: H Haapio and S Passaria, 'Improving Contract Clarity' (31 July 2014) (an excellent webinar presentation with accompanying notes) and H Haapio and S Passaria, 'Visual Law: What Lawyers Need To Learn From Information Designers' (15 May 2013).

SECTION 7: LOSING LEGALESE

CR Trudeau, 'The Public Speaks: An Empirical Study of Legal Communication' (May 20, 2012). 14 Scribes J. Leg. Writing 121 (2011-2012).

Garner's Dictionary of Legal Usage (Hardcover), Bryan Garner. See also a fun article on these 'here-and-there' words based on Garner's work by Andy Mergendahl (Lawyerist, 24 May 2012) lawyerist.com/43513/legal-writing-ditch-here-and-there-words/, accessed 10 June 2017.

J Kimble, 'You Think the Law Requires Legalese? (21 October 2013).

Centre for Plain Language, 'Law Words: 30 essays on legal words & phrases' (1995).

Law Reform Commission of Victoria, 'Plain English and the Law Report' (1987) No 9, Appendix I Drafting manual: Guidelines for drafting in plain English

Black's Law Dictionary (2nd Pocket Edition), definition via lawyerist.com/28922/thy-legal-writing-shall-not-include-shall/, accessed 10 June 2017.

J Kimble, 'What is plain language?' (2002).

BA Garner, 'Learning to Loathe Legalese' (November 2006).

JS Ammon, 'Indemnification: Banish the Word! And Rebuild Your Indemnity Clause from Scratch' (September 2013).

Plain English Campaign, 'The A to Z of alternative words' (2001).

DM Oppenheimer, 'Consequences of Erudite Vernacular Utilized Irrespective of Necessity: Problems with Using Long Words Needlessly' Applied Cognitive Psychology, (31 October 2005).

SECTION 8 & 9: PRODUCTIVE CONTRACT PROCESS & MAJOR MAPPING

GW Dent, 'Business Lawyers as Enterprise Architects' (2009). 64 The Business Lawyer 279 (2009); Case Legal Studies Research Paper No. 08-25.

Australian Story, 'She's Not There' (14 July 2008) Retrieved via abc.net.au/austory/content/2007/s2304453.htm, accessed 9 May 2017.

TD Barton, H Haapio and T Borisova, 'Flexibility and Stability in Contracts' (2014).

I also agree with fellow automation-lover Terry Walby from Thoughtonomy in disagreeing with Bill Gates to some degree. A little automation is better than no automation — even on an inefficient process. See T Walby 'Why Bill Gates was Wrong on Automation' (8 September 2015).

H Haapio, and DA Plewe, and R deRooy, 'Contract Continuum: From Text to Images, Comics, and Code' (February 23, 2017).

S McCoubrey, 'Can plain language change our approach to conflict' (November 2016) Presented at Clarity2016, Wellington, New Zealand. Retrieved via clarity2016.org/can-plain-language-change-our-approach-to-conflict, accessed 7 June 2017.

Mind Mapping, 'What is a Mind Map?'(2017).

Think Buzan, 'Mind Mapping Evidence Report'.

For 5 Why technique straight from Toyota, see toyota-global.com/company/toyota_traditions/quality/mar_apr_2006.html, accessed 27 May 2017.

Graphics in this book

Icons on pages 40, 74, 108, and 132 are from the Noun Project (https://thenounproject.com) and used under their Royalty-Free License.

Other icons and graphics are created by the author or created for the author by Lauren Frederiks from The Elise Design Collective (theelise.com.au)

Digital Resources

This book comes with further digital resources (sweet!).

For templates and checklists, head to: www.createcontractsclientslove.com

Scan the QR code to visit the Create Contracts Clients Love site and access included templates